# CALMING THE
# STORM WITHIN

### How to Find Peace in
### This Chaotic World

# Jim Lange

Forewords by
Ray Hilbert & Os Hillman

Published by Five Feet Twenty
PO Box 1
Lambertville, MI 48144
5feet20.com

ISBN 13: 978-0-9886137-0-6

ISBN 10: 0-9886137-0-0

Cover design by Jennifer Lassiter

*To my incredible parents...my mom who taught me that everything is a Not To Worry (or an NTW) and my dad who taught me the value of integrity.*

# Acknowledgments

Wow, where do I begin to thank all of those who were so helpful in making this book a reality?

First, I must thank my beautiful wife, Connie, who not only helped with proofreading but also patiently remained by my side through the long journey of writing. Thank you, Honey—I love you.

Thank you also to Rod Brant, Pete Nowka, Becky Robinson, Michele Howe, Chris Bonham, Jack Hollister, Mike Fisher and Jim Ross for your incredible insights and encouragement during different stages of this project. You helped to keep me going.

Kevin VanErt, thank you for opening up your "vault of knowledge" regarding Scripture and helping to keep me on track in certain areas of this book.

Dan Rogers, thank you for encouraging me to expand the section on embracing chaos. Your words were very well-timed and much appreciated.

Tiffany Colter and Grant Webster, thank you for your insight and coaching during the finishing stages of this book. You were both so helpful in getting me into position for launch.

Jennifer Lassiter, you did a masterful job on the cover design. Thank you for your patience with me and your attention to detail.

And a special thank you to Rod Brandt who spent considerable time editing and laying out this manuscript. I appreciate your help and your friendship more than you know.

Thank you also to two very special friends, Bob Borcherdt and Denise Emerine. Bob, your thoughts throughout the writing of this book were extremely helpful to me. I am forever grateful that you cared enough for me to tell me that you didn't think this book was ready. If it weren't for your boldness, I probably would have released this a year or more too soon. Denise, your prayers, encouragement and input along the way were so helpful—thank you!

I also want to thank you, the reader of this book for the confidence you have placed in me. I pray that you will be deeply impacted by the truth revealed in these pages and that you will truly discover the peace, which transcends all understanding.

But most of all, I want to thank my Father in Heaven who loves me dearly and walks with me each day. Thank You Abba, I love you!

# Endorsements

"This is the best book on attaining peace that I've ever read. Jim Lange takes us deep into the scriptural foundation for true peace and, through a transparent window into his personal life, gives us hope that we needn't spend our days in anxiety and worry. *Calming the Storm Within* has all the makings of a classic, but for now I recommend making it your personal and valued companion."

~ John D. Beckett
Chairman, The Beckett Companies
Author: *Loving Monday* and *Mastering Monday*

"Do you lack peace in your life? Then you need to read *Calming the Storm Within* by my friend Jim Lange. Jim provides a practical handbook on how to gain peace in the midst of painful life experiences using personal stories and biblical truths you can apply to your life. I found it an excellent resource in my life and know you will too."

~ Os Hillman
President, Marketplace Leaders
Author: *TGIF Today God Is First* and *Change Agent*

"If there's one commodity in great demand and short supply in our fast-paced, chaotic, unpredictable world, it's peace. Not only are nations warring against each other, but many of us are fighting an intense, internal war for inner peace. In *Calming the Storm Within*, Jim Lange has written an honest account of his own quest for peace, filled with examples from everyday life. In the process, he charts a practical, straight-forward path to peace we all can follow, using principles firmly anchored in timeless, tried and tested principles from the Scriptures."

~ Robert J. Tamasy
Author, editor, and Vice President of Communications,
Leaders Legacy, Inc.

"Like all of us, Jim Lange is no stranger to those seasons of life when stress and chaos can seem overpowering. Unlike many of us, Jim has discerned a spiritual path that cuts through clutter and brings us to a place of peace. This is a penetrating book of insights and applications for those seeking a more centered approach to life."

~ Chuck Proudfit
Founder and President,
At Work on Purpose

"Peace is a state of being that surpasses all the successes, _and_ all the sufferings of life. It's not just for the spiritually perfect or the chosen few. It's yours for the asking and the 'entering.' _Calming the Storm Within_ is your passport to discovering peace in this often painful world. Don't delay a day, read it now."

~ Harvey A. Hook
Author: _The Power of an Ordinary Life_

"I have read countless books on this subject matter in preparation for delivering sermons and I honestly didn't expect to be impressed, but impressed I was! In fact, with your permission I may use some of your highlights for sermon notes. I found the book to be: fresh, thought provoking, challenging, emotionally moving and encouraging. In addition, the way it's written makes it easy to make immediate life applications. Great job!"

~ Lee Powell
Senior Pastor, CedarCreek Church
Toledo, Ohio

"Jim Lange has created a dynamic and practical resource to guide readers seeking to know, understand, and experience God's peace...despite how they feel; despite uncertain circumstances, despite ever-changing world events. Lange does an excellent job helping Christ followers to fully embrace that peace promised to them by God...which does, indeed, pass all understanding. With lots of lively storytelling and personal examples, Lange leads readers from unbiblical to biblical thinking which powerfully changes lives from the inside out. Highly recommended for every person desiring stability in a highly unstable world."

~ Michele Howe
Author: *Burdens Do a Body Good:*
*Meeting Life's Challenges with Strength and Soul*

"Jim Lange lives a balanced life and speaks from healthy experience. All of us would benefit from his practical counsel and anecdotes on living at peace as outlined here. This book is accessible to folks from all walks of life."

~ Matthew A Thomas
Bishop, Free Methodist Church – USA

"Most people , if not all, are in pursuit of inner peace. However, many have yet to find it. We have heard that it is achievable, but we still find ourselves searching for it. Jim Lange has done an excellent job of describing what keeps us from peace and then shares a process of how we can truly experience inner peace...regardless of our circumstances. Jim, thank you for writing *Calming the Storm Within* –it has helped me and I know it will help many others!"

~ Ford Taylor
FSH Consulting Group, LLC
(Transformational Leadership the Missing Link)

"*Calming The Storm Within* is both practical and comprehensive. If we would all apply these principals, life would be much less chaotic and filled with the peace God wants us to enjoy—His peace!"

~ Bay Forrest
Evangelist and director of Focus Ministries

"Jim Lange has done us all a favor by writing *Calming the Storm Within* and sharing his considerable wisdom on finding peace and contentment in the ultra-chaotic and fast-paced world of the 21st century. Jim provides us with a biblically based game plan for handling the life challenges that frequently prevent us from experiencing the blessings of our Christian faith. This book is a must read for people who want to be better equipped to take life HEAD ON and really grow their faith!"

~ Clinton O. Longenecker, Ph. D.
Author, Speaker, Executive Coach
Stranahan Professor of Leadership and Organizational Excellence,
The College of Business and Organizational Excellence
at The University of Toledo

# Table of Contents

# Foreword

As one who consumes many books each year, one of the first questions I ask myself when contemplating whether to read a new book is whether the author has something unique to say. I'll also try to discern if they have written it to either complete an obligation to a publisher or to pad their own body of work. All too often, I find myself comparing what I am reading to other "similar" writings, and ultimately do not understand the driving motive that moved the author to write.

Not so with my dear friend Jim Lange's work, *Calming The Storm Within: How To Find Peace in This Chaotic World.*

Without question, we live in a troubled world and face crises never before seen by today's generation. As of the writing of this Foreword, our nation's debt has skyrocketed to over $16 trillion, unemployment figures remain historically high and median personal income has consistently declined over the last several years. At nearly every turn, the economic conditions are moving toward a cataclysmic fall. Uncertainty rules the day. Worry, fear, and doubt are overtaking many people. Integrity and commitment to a moral code of ethics are seemingly in the rear view mirror. In such difficult times in the past, people have historically turned to God and their traditional roots for comfort and assurance. But every report and indication that I see these days indicates just the opposite. Church attendance is down nearly everywhere, young people are abandoning traditional religious institutions at a record pace. Sexual impurity is rampant. Financial conservatism seems to be lost. I could continue. But in just four simple words I can sum it all up...The World Is Lost.

While this perfect storm of financial, moral, and ethical issues rages on, it is obvious that many people have no idea how to calm the growing anxiety they feel. They try many methods to feel better about things. Many buy things they cannot afford, with money they don't have, to impress people they don't really know or like in the first place. Some look to food for comfort. Others bury themselves in their work. Some become absorbed in television, alcohol, illicit drugs, or other means to escape their current reality. I suppose this has been the case since the beginning of the human race (after the "fall of man" in the Garden). And while these things may bring temporary "happiness" or fulfillment, any satisfaction from such shallow things soon leads to an even deeper sense of desperation and understanding that "something is missing."

What is it that these people are so desperately seeking to find that mysteriously continues to elude them? Peace.

So when I read Jim's book on this topic, I knew right away he had written something every person on this planet should read. And I was terribly honored and thrilled when he asked me to pen the foreword to his work.

Let me add this thought—no matter where you are in your personal spiritual journey—you need to read this book. Whether you are a sold out follower of Jesus Christ, someone who denies the very existence of God, or somewhere in between—you simply must read this book. Even if you don't believe what Jim has to say, and even if you want to argue with him on every point, you simply won't be able to deny that Jim has discovered what you—and every person on planet Earth seeks...Peace in a troubled world.

As you read this book, I want to encourage you to give yourself plenty of time for each chapter. Grab your highlighter. Grab your Bible (if you have one—if not, no worry as Jim takes you painstakingly through God's Word). This is an extremely exhaustive writing that if you will take your time and allow it all to sink in, I am absolutely convinced you will better understand how you too can experience true peace in this chaotic world.

Jim walks you through many examples of situations and individuals who have learned and experienced for themselves the core message of his book. He will help you develop practical tools, processes, and strategies to gain personal peace, to get a handle on the stress that at times consumes you.

My simple question is this, *by reading this book, what do you have to lose?*

You have much to gain...most importantly internal sanity that everything within you desperately craves.

Enjoy...and may you experience "Shalom."

Ray Hilbert
CEO, Truth@Work
Co-Author, International Best Seller,
*The Janitor-How An Unexpected Friendship
Transformed a CEO & His Company*

The Bible tells us that Satan's mission is to steal, kill and destroy. Peace of mind is one of those areas where I see he steals from people every day.

There are many things we can fret about. However, Jesus made a profound statement in John 14:27: "Peace I leave with you, my peace I give to you; not as the world gives do I give to you. Let not your heart be troubled, neither let it be afraid." The kind of peace Jesus spoke about was not the kind the world gives. His peace was very different.

It was the kind of peace that allowed Him to sleep in the midst of a storm when His disciples were fretting. It was a kind of peace that allowed Him to sit quietly in the Garden of Gethsemane before His crucifixion. Let's face it; this is a very different kind of peace He is speaking about.

Jesus had many situations where He could have lost His peace. He had a busy schedule and many constantly vied for His attention. Everyone wanted a piece of Him.

Over the years, I have discovered that there is a bridge each of us must cross to get to peace and it's called faith. It is impossible to gain peace in the midst of any kind of traumatic event without knowing and experiencing the presence of God in our lives. That involves faith. John 8:32 says "the truth shall make you free." It is knowing the truth about the nature of the One who holds the keys to every solution to life's problems that allows us to appropriate peace in the midst of every life circumstance. The moment we question the nature of God and His activity in our lives, peace is soon to evaporate. We've lost faith in the One who has the key to giving us peace.

I've known Jim for many years now. I met him at a marketplace event and I've watched Jim embrace truth and apply it in his life. I've seen him grow in his love and service of our Lord. The book you hold in your hand is the fruit of this growth. God has given Jim insights about what it means to walk in peace no matter the circumstance.

I've discovered that Satan wants to kill our destiny in many ways. However, if we are successful in overcoming his attacks, whatever God sets us free from, He automatically gives us an anointing to set other people free from the very thing we were a victim of. He not only delivers us from what the enemy has done in our lives, He actually gives us an anointing in the area we used to be a victim to. He turns that into our ministry. Our vengeance on the enemy is to set other people free from the very thing he victimized us with.

This book is the fruit of this victory over Satan. Jim gives us some very practical application about how to acquire peace. He now has the authority to share this because it is his payback to the enemy of our souls who seeks to rob every human of their peace.

Do you lack peace in your life? *Calming the Storm Within* provides a practical handbook on how to gain peace in the midst of painful life experiences using personal stories and biblical truths you can apply to your life.

Os Hillman
President, Marketplace Leaders
Author, *TGIF Today God Is First* and *Change Agent*

# Introduction to Peace

What is peace and why is it so important? Is chaos a bad thing or can it be good? What are some of the things that can rob us of peace? Can we truly find peace in our lives and if so, how? We will answer all of these questions and more as we begin our journey together.

Here is what we will explore in the coming chapters...

# The Peace I Want

*An anxious heart weighs a man down.*
*Proverbs 12:25a*

*"He is happiest, be the king or peasant,*
*who finds peace in his home."*
*Goethe*

Horatio G. Spafford (1828-1888) was a successful attorney in Chicago who was also a devout Christian. Spafford is best known for having written the well-known hymn, *It is Well With My Soul.*

In 1871, a fire in Chicago devastated the city. Just months before, Spafford had invested heavily in real estate and the disaster wiped out his financial holdings. To make matters worse, Spafford's only son died during this time.

Two years later, he planned a trip to Europe for himself, his wife, and their four daughters so they could get some much-needed rest. He was also planning to help D.L. Moody during one of his evangelistic campaigns while in Great Britain.

Because of a last-minute business transaction he needed to address, he was not able to travel with his family. He sent them on ahead with the promise that he would be a few days behind them.

On November 22nd of that year, the ship carrying his wife and daughters collided with another ship. Miraculously his wife was saved when her unconscious body happened to rest upon a floating plank. However, their four daughters all passed away.

When his wife came ashore, she wired her husband with only two words, "Saved alone." So a grief-stricken Spafford began the journey across the ocean to meet his brokenhearted bride. On the way, he was called up to the deck and was told by the captain that according to his calculations, they were directly over the spot that claimed the lives of his daughters.

Spafford solemnly retreated to his cabin and penned the words to this wonderful song:

## It Is Well With My Soul

When peace, like a river, attendeth my way,
When sorrows like sea billows roll;
Whatever my lot, Thou has taught me to say,
It is well, it is well, with my soul.

*It is well, with my soul,*
*It is well, with my soul,*
*It is well, it is well, with my soul.*

Though Satan should buffet, though trials should come,
Let this blest assurance control,
That Christ has regarded my helpless estate,
And hath shed His own blood for my soul.

*It is well, with my soul,*
*It is well, with my soul,*
*It is well, it is well, with my soul.*

My sin, oh, the bliss of this glorious thought!
My sin, not in part but the whole,
Is nailed to the cross, and I bear it no more,
Praise the Lord, praise the Lord, O my soul!

*It is well, with my soul,*
*It is well, with my soul,*
*It is well, it is well, with my soul.*

And Lord, haste the day when my faith shall be sight,
The clouds be rolled back as a scroll;
The trump shall resound, and the Lord shall descend,
Even so, it is well with my soul.

*It is well, with my soul,*
*It is well, with my soul,*
*It is well, it is well, with my soul.*

How a man like Spafford could write such words, "It is well with my soul," in the midst of such incredible pain is unfathomable to me. However, he obviously had something that many of us long for. He had a peace that went beyond his circumstances. A peace that I have longed for all my life.

I believe God laid the idea for this book on my heart so I could write it, not only for you, but mostly for me. Don't get me wrong, I have come a long way...but I have a distance yet to go.

In fact, though I have learned much about finding peace, I am not writing this from the position of "expert" at all. Quite the opposite. This was born from a lifelong quest for peace that, at most times, has seemed unsuccessful. I am now seeing it as a journey I have been on, and am continuing on. I clearly don't have all the answers and I am not saying that what is written here is an all-encompassing solution to the lack of peace many of us feel. However, there is some great wisdom here that will guide you along your path to peace.

Growing up, I worried about everything. I worried about striking out in a baseball game and letting my teammates down, whether I'd miss the bus to school, whether I'd shoot too much in a basketball game and have my teammates think I was a ball hog or if I said something stupid, that others wouldn't like me.

Often, my worry (or fear) would paralyze me. It would cause me to take no action whatsoever. I distinctly remember times in high school, wanting to ask a girl out on a date and just staring at the phone before dialing. *What if she says "No"?* I couldn't handle the rejection so I would agonizingly stare at the phone for days and do nothing.

I found that peace was eluding me and I didn't like it one bit so I tried to create my own peace. I became a list maker. I would make a list of all the things I needed to get done. I found that when I completed something on my list and was able to check it off, it gave me great satisfaction...a type of peace. If I would do something that wasn't on my list, sometimes I would actually add the task to my list just so I would have the satisfaction of crossing it off. A pretty sad case, huh?

While playing basketball in college, I recall being so nervous prior to games that I would get sick to my stomach. I would say to myself, *Your career is almost over. After basketball is done, you won't have anything else to get nervous about ever again.* How foolish I was! To think that nervousness and worry would go away after my college days!

If anything upset my ordered world, I would lose my peace. The problem was that the world didn't care much about my level of peace and it did not cooperate very often. It seemed that I was constantly in this state of turmoil and stress. In the coming pages I will share the rest of my story including something that was a "game changer" for me.

## Even Tough Times Are Good

Many nights when my family is able to eat dinner together, we go around the table sharing our "Highs and Lows." We each take turns telling about the worst thing that happened to us (our low) that day followed by the best thing that happened (our high).

A while back, something unique happened. My daughter Kristin, who was in her last year of nursing school, said that her high and low was both the same thing. She had taken a final exam that morning at 8 a.m., for which she had been studying tirelessly. For some reason her alarm clock did not wake her; the sound was turned way down. She arose at 8 a.m., the exact start time of her exam! And, because she was living at home, she was about 20-25 minutes away from the college. She raced around, whipped her hair into a pony tail and brushed her teeth. Thankfully, my wife Connie was home and she prayed with Kristin before sending her on her way out the door.

Kristin arrived very late and calmly took her exam. She said that though she was 45 minutes late, she finished her exam before many of her classmates. She said she had a very clear mind and thought she did well on her final.

Upon hearing this, three things immediately came to mind:

1. There is incredible power in prayer;
2. It is very important to be prepared (which Kristin was);
3. Our troubles can actually turn out to be victories when we let God enter in.

We may not see that victory immediately, but it will eventually happen if we love God and are called according to His purpose (see Romans 8:28). Let's look at how Jesus modeled peace to us in the midst of chaos:

> Then he got into the boat and his disciples followed him. Without warning, a furious storm came up on the lake, so that the waves swept over the boat. But Jesus was sleeping. The disciples went and woke him, saying, "Lord, save us!

We're going to drown!"
He replied, "You of little faith, why are you so afraid?"
Then he got up and rebuked the winds and the waves, and it
was completely calm. (Matthew 8:23-26)

What an interesting passage! In my book, *Bleedership: Biblical
First-Aid for Leaders,* I shared this:

> Have you ever been in a boat when waves were coming
> over the side? It can be very frightening. Let's look at how
> Jesus reacted a little more closely.
> What was He doing at this time? He was sleeping! Other
> than death, I challenge you to come up with a more calm
> state than sleeping. I think that Jesus *chose* to be sleeping at
> this time, as He wanted to show us how at peace He really
> was, so that we could learn from Him.[1]

That's the peace I want, the level of peace where in every situation I can know in my heart that God's got it figured out. In Kristin's
situation, it all worked out for good and that became apparent in
only a couple of hours. In most situations, however, we don't see a
conclusion for quite some time and we might fret about our circumstances. I want to be so filled with peace that I can truly believe
that everything is going to work out for good.

Several years ago, I was asked to be the chairman of our city's
19th annual National Day of Prayer Breakfast. This is a great event
in our region and is typically sold-out each year with close to 1,000
people in attendance.

One of my primary jobs involved securing a speaker for the event.
So, a year in advance, I reached out to someone I had met who was
very well known in the "faith in the workplace" world.

He gladly agreed to speak at the event and we signed a contract
to seal the deal. Five months before the event, I received a call from
his assistant informing me that because of a pressing matter he

would not be able to speak on that date. Our speaker was the vice president of an international not-for-profit organization and the president had just resigned. That made him the president by default and he was needed in Jerusalem to lead a meeting on the same day as our prayer breakfast.

I felt as if I had been hit in the stomach. My main job...to get a speaker. And now we had no one. I immediately emailed our committee and received a response from one of my cohorts that impacted me. His response went something like this, "Well, I guess God didn't want him as our speaker this year and He must have someone better in mind."

My immediate thought after reading it was, *I wish I'd said that!* Deep down, what I was really thinking was, *I wish I had such strong faith.*

To complete the story, we ended up bringing in Ray Hilbert, the founder of Truth@Work in Indianapolis, as our speaker. He did a wonderful job and deeply impacted those in attendance in profound ways that morning. Immediately after the breakfast, Ray and I went to a local restaurant to get to know one another. We talked for about three hours and it was very clear to me that we were supposed to be working together. This feeling was so strong that at many points during our conversation I actually wept uncontrollably (strange, but true). Clearly God had ordained this appointment.

This encounter led to me become chapter president for Truth@Work (christianroundtablegroups.com) in Northwest Ohio and Southeast Michigan. In this role I have been so blessed to be able to see God do some truly amazing things and I am so thankful that I have the opportunity to serve in this capacity. I am still amazed by the way God worked things out for good, even when things looked hopeless for a long while.

## So Be It

In the book, *Pray Big* by Will Davis Jr., I was first introduced to the phrase, "So Be It person."[2] This is someone who says, "So be it" regardless of their circumstances. They understand that God is in control and they have faith that He knows what they need far better than they do. Because of this, they are OK no matter what is going on around them. They are a So Be It person.

From that point on, that phrase has stuck with me and it is one of my regular prayers, that God would change my heart so that I would be a So Be It person.

To be funny, a friend of mine once said, "If you can remain calm, then you just don't have all the facts." Well, I want to have all the facts, even if they are not pretty, and still be able to calmly say, "So be it."

It is this yearning, to be a So Be It Christ-follower, to be at peace regardless of my circumstances, which has led me to write this book. It is my prayer that the tools and insights presented here might bless you in some way and help you, too, on your path to becoming a So Be It person.

By the way, after our prayers we always say, "Amen," right? Do you know what the word "Amen" means? "So be it."

## Receive or Go Get?

Bob is a dear friend of mine. He and I get together at least once every two weeks to "do life" together. He and I go way back and were college basketball teammates for three years. (He is a year younger than me, which he reminds me of often).

One of the things I love about Bob is that he is a very deep thinker. He challenges me frequently in very healthy ways and helps me stretch my mind, and my heart. During one of our times together, we were discussing the subject of peace and he shared one of his thoughts that made me say, "Huh. That's a great question." An interesting discussion followed; the following are some of the excerpts from that time together.

Bob said, "As I was thinking about the subject of peace, I couldn't answer a question that has been bugging me. Is peace given to us or is it something we need to go get?"

Though I hadn't thought about it in those terms, I knew where he was going. We immediately went to some verses which, on the surface, appear to contradict themselves.

In John 14:27a, Jesus said, "Peace I leave with you; my peace I give you." So clearly, peace is given.

Yet, Psalm 34:14b tells us that we are to "seek peace and pursue it."

So what gives? Do we receive it or go get it?

Yes. We must do both. God's Word shows us that: 1) the only way to have true peace is to be open to receiving it from God; and 2) that once we are open to receiving it, we must actually **do** something to get it, we must seek it or pursue it.

I know this will ruffle some feathers, but the Scriptures clearly show that we don't get peace from doing nothing. Can we find peace by doing nothing? Sure. Is it okay to do nothing? Of course. I'm not implying otherwise. I mean that peace does not come by *only* doing nothing. Just for clarity, the **doing** I'm referring to is not a bunch of tasks, rather it is choosing the attitude of your heart and choosing whom you will serve and love, which we will discuss in the coming pages.

## Why Seek Peace?

Come, my children, listen to me; I will teach you the fear of the LORD. Whoever of you loves life and desires to see many good days, keep your tongue from evil and your lips from speaking lies. Turn from evil and do good; *seek peace and pursue it.* (Psalm 34:11-14, emphasis added)

The Psalmist who wrote the verses above is telling those who would like "to see many good days" to:
- Keep our tongues from evil;
- Not lie;
- Turn from evil;

- Do good;
- Seek and pursue peace.

(Note: these verses also appear in the New Testament in 1 Peter 3:10-12)

So, if you love life and desire to see many good days, seeking and pursuing peace is one of the things you will do.

---

**Takeaway:**
*Peace is something provided to us by God (which we need to both seek and receive) that enables us to have tranquility, or be okay on the inside, regardless of our circumstances.*

## Prayer

Dear Lord, please help me understand this thing You have made available to each of us...this thing called "peace." I desperately want more peace, Father, and I thank You for making it so readily available. Help me to seek it out and to go get it, while at the same time receive it from You. I don't want to rely on my circumstances to determine the level of peace in my life. Please help me to be a So Be It person, someone who is at peace regardless of what is happening in my life. Open my heart to what You have to say to me as I read this book. Thank you Lord! Amen.

---

# TWO

# Embrace the Chaos

*Consider it pure joy, my brothers, whenever you face trials*
*of many kinds because you know that the testing of your faith*
*develops perseverance. Perseverance must finish its work so*
*that you may be mature and complete, not lacking anything.*
James 1:2-4

*"You cannot find peace by avoiding life."*
*Virginia Woolf*

According to *Wikipedia*, "inner peace" (peace of mind) refers to a state of being mentally and spiritually at peace, with enough knowledge and understanding to keep oneself strong in the face of discord or stress. Being "at peace" is considered by many to be healthy and the opposite of being stressed or anxious. Peace of mind is generally associated with bliss, happiness and contentment.

An antonym for inner peace is chaos. Chaos can appear in the form of anything that naturally moves us from peace. This can include circumstances that produce turmoil, pain, discomfort, stress, trouble, etc... With that being said, it's only logical to assume that in order to live a life at peace, chaos must be avoided or at least reduced, right? That is obviously not correct, but that's exactly what I have spent the majority of my life doing, trying to avoid chaos. I thought all chaos was bad. What a mistake!

Not only is it not true that we should be avoiding chaos, it's not possible. One of the promises Jesus made to us is that we would all have trouble in this life (see John 16:33), so it is imperative that we embrace trouble, or chaos. The sooner we can come to a place of understanding about the positive role chaos can play in our lives, the sooner we will be on the path to peace...peace in the midst of our chaos.

Chaos is sometimes a consequence of something we have done. Other times chaos ensues when we have done nothing to bring it on. One instance could be when our enemy, Satan, tries to disrupt us (which we will also touch on a bit later). Another case is when God allows chaos to enter our lives for our own good; first, to turn us to His Son and second, to prune us to be more like Jesus and so that we are more productive in what He has called us to. This is exactly what God has done and is continuing to do in me.

In the 1990's I found myself in a position that many would like to be in, at least those looking from the outside. I had a healthy, growing family. My career was taking off and I was making more money than I thought possible. We were buying things...we were taking vacations...we were saving money...we had it all. Except peace. During those years I had more stress in my life than at any time I can remember and I couldn't understand this because this was not the way it was supposed to work. I grew up believing that money was the goal...the more you made and saved, the more security you would have—and presumably the more peace you'd have. But I was finding this to not be true. Chaos was my life.

I finally came to a point where I said, *something's got to change!* I went to the library and checked out books on relaxation through meditation. I practiced this for a while and it did seem to help a little; however, I knew that something was still missing. What I have since discovered is that, while there is nothing wrong with relaxation, it is only temporary and very much a product of your circumstances. Though I didn't realize it, what I was really searching for was inner peace. I wanted something that would be with me *regardless* of my circumstances.

I considered myself a Christian because I regularly attended church and served on different committees there. I was doing "good" things and thought, *if anyone's a Christian, I am!* I was practically breaking my arm patting myself on the back.

Then something happened that I will discuss in chapter 5 which allowed me to see things differently...I had a breakthrough. That day I made a commitment to follow Jesus—something I had never done before.

## Christ-Followers are Unstable

When we commit our lives to follow Jesus, we execute a transaction in which we immediately become unstable. Peter describes it this way:

> Praise be to the God and Father of our Lord Jesus Christ! In his great mercy he has given us new birth into a living hope through the resurrection of Jesus Christ from the dead, and into an inheritance that can never perish, spoil or fade— kept in heaven for you, who through faith are shielded by God's power until the coming of the salvation that is ready to be revealed in the last time. In this you greatly rejoice, *though now for a little while you may have had to suffer grief in all kinds of trials. These have come so that your faith—of greater worth than gold, which perishes even though refined by fire—may be proved genuine and may result in praise, glory and honor when Jesus Christ is revealed.* (1 Peter 1:3-7, emphasis added)

When we enter into this relationship with Jesus, we are given an awesome inheritance in heaven that can never go away and we are also given protection by God's power. In exchange for this, we must trade our life for Jesus' life. Jesus is very clear to us that His life is not the easy life (see Matthew 8:19-22). In the above passage, Peter says that we may have to suffer grief in all kinds of trials for two reasons:

1. So that our faith can be refined, or purified like gold, which requires intense heat;
2. And so that our faith can be proved genuine.

Chaos, trouble and trials are not fun, but they are needed in our lives. Without them, we would not be able to grow into the people that God made us to become. We would fall short of our potential—we would not be all we can be.

Jesus' brother James tells us this concerning our troubles:

> Consider it pure joy, my brothers, whenever you face trials of many kinds, because you know that the testing of your faith develops perseverance. Perseverance must finish its work so that you may be mature and complete, not lacking anything. (James 1:2-4)

Jesus paints the picture of a gardener when teaching on this subject:

> "I am the true vine, and my Father is the gardener. He cuts off every branch in me that bears no fruit, while every branch that does bear fruit he prunes so that it will be even more fruitful." (John 15:1-2)

In this picture, Jesus is telling us that the gardener is God Himself. And, He will prune us so that we will be more fruitful or productive. In other words, it is for our own good! Jesus also warns that those branches that don't bear fruit will be lopped off. So why would we not want to bear fruit? We're going to get cut either way!

However you look at it, as refining or pruning, the fact is that it is painful. But, it is also for our own good. God loves us so much that He will allow chaos to occur in our lives...so we can move away from our comfort zones.

## Robert and Martial Arts

At this writing, my son Robert is 15. He, like most of us, really likes his comfort zone. From a very early age, he hasn't liked trying anything new, including foods. I would estimate that more than 95 percent of the time though, when he has finally tried something, he has gotten a sheepish grin on his face and said something like, "I *do* like it."

The same is true with activities. Because he is one who likes routine and because of some negative experiences on the baseball diamond and basketball court, he is pretty content to stay inside and watch TV or play video games...that is his comfort zone.

A couple of years ago I told Robert that I wanted him doing something physical. He said, "There's nothing to do that I like." I recognized that what he was really saying was, "I don't want to try anything new, I'm happy right here."

Several people had encouraged me to have him try mixed martial arts so I arranged to have him try this. On the way to the facility, he was extremely agitated with me and told me that he was sure he would hate it. When we arrived, he was so mad that he wouldn't even look the instructor in the eyes. The instructor suggested that Robert and I do a little sparring and he put us through the paces. I could tell Robert was enjoying this. Afterward he asked my son what he thought and Robert responded, "It was okay...at least it was better than I thought it was going to be." Again, what I sensed he was really saying was, "I liked it, but I can't say that because I thought I would hate it."

So, for two years now he has been taking classes for a couple hours per week. He often doesn't want to go because the sessions are demanding and sometimes painful; however, immediately afterward he tells me he is so glad he went. This process is helping him to gain in skill and in confidence. He is growing. However, in this case, it took me, his dad, to push him into it. If left to himself, Robert would stay at home. The fact is that I love my son so much that I am willing to push him into this "pain" so that he can get better and grow. The same is true with our heavenly Dad and us. He will allow us to experience pain, trouble and chaos because He loves us so much and He knows how this will help us.

## Other Positives of Pain

As I will share more about later, the fact is that there are consequences to our actions. When we don't follow God's way and we go off on our own, we pay the price. However, living righteously does not mean we will have a life of tranquility, free from pain and chaos. No one lived a more righteous life than Jesus. Yet, He suffered more than anyone ever will. Another example is a man named Job who is described in this manner:

> In the land of Uz there lived a man whose name was Job. This man was blameless and upright; he feared God and shunned evil. (Job 1:1)

He was blameless and upright. However, you probably know his story. Despite living right, he endured pain that I cannot even imagine and his life was turned totally upside down. In the midst of this chaos and pain, his "friends" wondered what evil he had done to make God bring this upon him. Like Job's friends, I have had thoughts that if I can just live right and do the right things, then I can avoid pain and chaos—a huge lie. The truth we all must come to grips with is that righteous living, while being very good for us, doesn't get us off the hook. There are many benefits in seeking righteousness, but avoiding pain and chaos is not one of them.

While this is a bit scary, it doesn't have to be. Understanding this means you can live with the bigger picture in mind. Just like when you go in for surgery, you know there will be pain, but you also know that it will eventually be good for you. It is all in your attitude.

Pain and trials are never fun. However, they are good for us in that they can steer us toward Jesus. They produce perseverance, which helps us to be more mature. They refine, or prune us. But there are more benefits. Pain in our lives also helps to steer us toward righteousness and peace.

> No discipline seems pleasant at the time, but painful. Later on, however, *it produces a harvest of righteousness and peace* for those who have been trained by it. (Hebrews 12:11, emphasis added)

While playing college basketball, I remember a stretch of time in which I just couldn't make a lay-up. Yes, that's right, there was about a week or two when I experienced this mental block and I couldn't make a "bunny" (and I'm 6'8" tall or as I like to say 5'20"—that's why my website is 5feet20.com). Put me 15-20 feet from the basket and I was fine, but up close, I fell apart.

During one practice, we were running through our "press breaker." This was what we did when our opponent would put a full-court press on us and guard us the entire length of the court. We tried to turn this into an opportunity to score quickly. I was typically assigned to the position under our basket, probably because I was one of the slowest on the team (but I made up for it by not being able to jump very high!). As the ball was passed from teammate to teammate, I was to position myself for an easy layup. During practice, my teammates were executing their portion flawlessly and getting the ball to me so I could score. However, I repeatedly would clang it off the rim. My coach and my teammates were not very happy with me.

They were all offering input to help me but I was not very open to it. I thought to myself, *Come on, this is a lay-up, the simplest shot there is. How much instruction do I need?* I was determined to fix my issue on my own, probably because of my embarrassment and pride.

Finally, my coach couldn't take it anymore and announced, "Okay, for each lay-up that Lange misses from here on out, all of you will be running a line drill." (This was a very unpleasant running exercise which was often used as "discipline.") All of my teammates groaned and I felt incredible pressure.

The next couple of times I still missed, so we ran. I remember a few of my teammates continuing to encourage me and offer suggestions. Now, because of the discipline we were receiving, I was eager for anything that may have been of help. I was finally open to receiving instruction to help me out of my slump. Thankfully, I eventually began to make my shots and regain my confidence. I can't remember what it was that helped me turn it around, but I can tell you this: I was driven to change, so driven that I would even accept coaching from my teammates on making this silly little shot.

I did **not** want to run anymore and I especially didn't want my teammates running because of me. That was very painful. But, I believe it was that pain that helped me get to a point of being willing to accept the teaching that got me out of my slump faster.

It's a fact that most of the time we must experience discipline in our lives in order for us to change our ways. This could come in any number of ways including correction from a friend, a rebuke, embarrassment, or pain in our lives. When was the last time that discipline was fun? As previously mentioned in Hebrews 12:11, no discipline is pleasant at the time, however, look at what it produces in us down the road...righteousness AND peace!

The book of Proverbs is known as the book of wisdom. Much of it was written by Solomon, who is acknowledged by many as the wisest man who ever lived. Check out these proverbs about discipline and correction:

> My son, do not despise the LORD's discipline and do not
> resent his rebuke, because the LORD disciplines those he loves,

as a father the son he delights in. (Proverbs 3:11-12)

He will die for lack of discipline, led astray by his own great folly. (Proverbs 5:23)

For these commands are a lamp, this teaching is a light, and the corrections of discipline are the way to life. (Proverbs 6:23)

He who heeds discipline shows the way to life, but whoever ignores correction leads others astray. (Proverbs 10:17)

Whoever loves discipline loves knowledge, but he who hates correction is stupid. (Proverbs 12:1)

He who ignores discipline comes to poverty and shame, but whoever heeds correction is honored. (Proverbs 13:18)

A fool spurns his father's discipline, but whoever heeds correction shows prudence. (Proverbs 15:5)

Stern discipline awaits him who leaves the path; he who hates correction will die. (Proverbs 15:10)

A mocker resents correction; he will not consult the wise. (Proverbs 15:12)

He who ignores discipline despises himself, but whoever heeds correction gains understanding. (Proverbs 15:32)

Jesus' closest followers were called disciples. A disciple is a pupil or a learner. One way to look at being disciplined is to be dedicated to being a disciple and open to correction or learning. So do you think God thinks it's important for us to be disciplined in our lives? I think so, too!

Here are a few great questions to ask yourself:

- Do I welcome discipline and correction? Or when corrected am I usually defensive?
- Who in my life knows they have an open invitation to correct me when they see I need it?
- Am I asking God regularly to search my heart (see Psalm 139:23) and show me where I need correction?

We are wired to avoid painful things like discipline, but God's

Word clearly states that we are to seek correction and embrace discipline. Though this is difficult, remember there is a huge payoff with this...righteousness and peace. I think it's worth the price!

## So Embrace It

We all desire inner peace. It is because of this desire, whether we have decided to follow Jesus or not, that God allows chaos (pain, turmoil, trouble) in our lives. He knows that the only place to find true peace is through Him. Hopefully, the chaos in our lives draws us closer to Him, where we can find true peace.

Therefore, it is imperative that we learn to embrace the chaos. Know that it is for our good...to help us. Simply knowing this should help us to overcome whatever we encounter, regardless of how chaotic it may be.

While knowing the reason for chaos and embracing it is critical and can help in our quest for inner peace, there is much more. The rest of this book will be dedicated to discovering how to have inner peace in the midst of our chaos. First, let's look at some of the things that steal our peace.

 **Takeaway:**
*Chaos is a part of life that cannot be avoided. We need to actually embrace the chaos because God allows it for our own good.*

## Prayer

Heavenly Father, thank You for loving me so much that You would allow chaos and trouble in my life. You know what I need and You know that staying in my comfort zone is not good for me. Help me to remember this the next time I face chaos and to be thankful in the midst of the storm. Help me to see it from Your vantage point so that I can choose peace in the midst of it and I can be looking for You during the turmoil. Amen.

# THREE

# Peace Stealers

*Cast all your anxiety on him because he cares for you.*
*1 Peter 5:7*

*"If I had my life to live over, I would perhaps have more*
*actual troubles but I'd have fewer imaginary ones."*
*Don Herold*

I recently discovered a lie I've believed. A counselor helped me see that I believed I was largely responsible for my wife's happiness. This false belief led to some unhealthy behavior on my part. If I said something that would upset Connie, I would immediately go into "fix it" mode. Because she wasn't "happy," I believed that I needed to change her mood. This created a great deal of anxiety in me as I was trying to control something that was outside of my control.

You see, until recently, my definition of success had been about the outcome. When I was an athlete, I was successful if I won the game. When I was in sales, high sales numbers made me a success.

In my marriage, a happy wife meant I was a good husband. Because of this belief, when I would sense Connie's unhappiness, I would stop at almost nothing until she was happy. This was exhausting for me...and for her!

Since coming to this realization, when I disagree with my wife or say something that upsets her, I do my best to let that be her problem (provided I'm not being a jerk, which does happen from time to time). Connie has told me that when I am able to do this and simply leave it between her and God, it helps her tremendously. During these times, she says that God usually shows her the truth. Sometimes she even thanks me for not trying to fix her and allowing God to work on her. Connie wanting this from me shows me that she is desiring to be more Christ-like in all she does and that when I don't get this right, I am actually robbing her of that opportunity to grow.

And you want to know who else is helped when I do this? Me! I have found freedom as I have come to realize that I can't control how my wife (or anyone else) feels or reacts; I can only control myself. I would love to tell you that I get this right 100 percent of the time, but that wouldn't be truthful—but I am getting better! Many times I am more like this man. He was a new patient in a doctor's office and the doctor remarked about his new patient's extraordinarily ruddy complexion. The patient said, "High blood pressure, Doc—it runs in my family."

"Your mother's side or your father's?" the doctor asked.

"Neither," the patient replied. "It's from my wife's family."

"Oh, come now." said the doctor, "How could your wife's family give you high blood pressure?"

The man sighed, "You oughta meet 'em sometime, Doc!"

As mentioned earlier, I have allowed my peace to be stolen many, many times in my life. I am presently on a quest to stop that and I am much more peaceful now than ever before...so I am making progress. However, there is one thing that still gives me problems...my schedule. But God is really working on me in this area. Remember, I love progress and I love to cross things off my list. So, when I don't get everything done on my schedule, I have a tendency to become agitated and, as a result, not very peaceful.

When I take a step back to analyze this, I really don't have a "schedule" problem; I have a "control" problem rooted in fear. I want to be in control of my day—everything in my day—because I am fearful of being overwhelmed. When something crops up that is unexpected, it can wreck my entire schedule. If I'm not careful, I can then allow this to steal my peace. Can you relate? There is a big problem when you need your day to go just right in order to have peace because your day rarely, if ever, goes according to plan!

A friend of mine asked me, "If someone spits on you does that make you mad?"

I said, "You bet!"

He challenged me and said, "No it doesn't, it only makes you wet. It is your choice to get angry." I wanted to dispute him, but he was right. He had me. In all cases, we choose our response.

In the same way, when evaluating my schedule, I could say that I'm so busy and stressed out and that's why I don't have peace. I could say that others, those "demanding" people, are causing this stress in my life...through their phone calls, appointments and emails (in other words, my schedule or others are "spitting on me" causing my stress). However, I've come to the realization that *I* am the one responsible for my lack of peace. How I react to any given situation is my choice and I **don't** have to give away my peace. After all, I'm the one who makes my schedule and I can choose to make it as busy or not busy as I would like.

In this situation, and in any other in which I feel anxious, my eyes are focused on my problem, my comfort, and me rather than on Jesus. I want to say that again. **Any lack of peace that I experience is simply because I am focusing on my issues and me rather than on Jesus.** The same is true for you. Here is a story of someone else who had the same problem:

> During the fourth watch of the night Jesus went out to them, walking on the lake. When the disciples saw him walking on the lake, they were terrified. "It's a ghost," they said, and cried out in fear.
>
> But Jesus immediately said to them: "Take courage! It is I. Don't be afraid."
>
> "Lord, if it's you," Peter replied, "tell me to come to you on the water."
>
> "Come," he said.
>
> Then Peter got down out of the boat, walked on the water and came toward Jesus. But *when he saw the wind, he was afraid* and, beginning to sink, cried out, "Lord, save me!"
>
> Immediately Jesus reached out his hand and caught him. "You of little faith," he said, "why did you doubt?" (Matthew 14:25-31, emphasis added)

When Peter was focused on Jesus, he was fine. It was when he "saw the wind," or when he took his eyes off Jesus that he became afraid and began to sink. Our peace can only be stolen when we take our eyes off Jesus.

The title of this chapter is "Peace Stealers," but it probably should have been "Those Things that Happen that Cause Us to Take Our Eyes Off Jesus." Not quite as catchy, but certainly more accurate.

## Other Peace Stealers

As mentioned, our peace cannot be stolen without our consent. It is our choice, to take our eyes off Jesus, which allows this. Here is a short list of some common things that can cause us to make this choice. This is not meant to be an all-inclusive list, but rather just a few general examples of what might trigger us to give our peace away. (For some detailed examples and some faith-building tips on dealing with each, please go to Appendix C, *Common Peace Stealers,* which can be found at calmingthestormwithin.com/appendix.)

· **Worry**

Worry can consume our thoughts and immobilize us. It can negatively affect relationships, diminish productivity and even damage our health.

· **Stress**

There is good stress and there is bad stress. I am talking about bad stress here. It can come from worry, feeling overwhelmed, trying to do too much, running late, trying to keep something hidden, or a lack of sleep, among other things.

· **Anger**

Anger can come when things don't go according to our plan. It could be triggered by something as simple as waiting on a tardy friend at a restaurant or a child's incompliant behavior.

· **Unforgiveness**

Unforgiveness takes place when we feel we have been wronged and we refuse to extend grace to the offending party. Not forgiving is like drinking poison and hoping the other person will die...not only is it unhealthy for us, it rarely affects the offending person.

· **Insecurity**

Feeling as if we don't measure up, feeling "less than," or trying to "prove" ourselves to others.

· **Not Following God**

The only way we can grow is to get out of our comfort zones, areas we don't naturally like to stray from. God continually wants us to grow and He will regularly prompt us to step out of our familiar and comfortable places. When we choose to ignore these promptings we stop following God and we agree to let our peace be taken. As we will discuss in the coming chapters, without God it is impossible to have peace. I have a friend who recently approached me and said, "I need your help. I'm feeling very far away from God and I don't know what to do." He was stirred to approach me because of the lack of peace he felt in his heart. He knew he was not where God wanted Him.

Consider some of your specific peace stealers. What have you allowed, or are you currently allowing, to steal your peace? I encourage you to write them down. Come on...do it right now in the lines below. (For a more specific list of some common peace stealers, see Appendix C at calmingthestormwithin.com/appendix.)

_____

_____

_____

How can you turn these over to God? What steps can you take on a daily basis to open your life to God's healing in this area? Will you trust God and release the outcome to Him?

Just like in the example I shared about my schedule, I would like to propose that each and every one of our peace stealers is really a control problem or an issue rooted in selfishness and ultimately, in fear. Each issue, and any other thing that causes us to lose our peace, really can be boiled down to the fact that we are trying to control the situation and that we are fretting when it does not go the way we want. Like Peter, we are focusing on the wind rather than on Jesus.

Review the list with me again and see if you don't agree:

- Worry is really saying, "I want to control the outcome by stewing about it even though I have no control over it." Worry is a form of arrogance, thinking that we know better or more than God.
- Stress is really saying, "I want to control my surroundings, my schedule, etc..."
- Anger is really saying, "This isn't how I planned it...I'm not in control anymore!"
- Unforgiveness is really saying, "Because you wronged me, I want to control you through my feelings and the way I treat you in return."

- Insecurity is really saying, "I want to control how others think of me."
- Not following God's leading is really saying, "I want to be the one in control of my life."

The common denominator here is that each of these instances reeks of an "It's all about me!" attitude. In other words, selfishness is the culprit which leads to a desire to control. In my case, the only time I tend to lose my peace is when things don't go the way **I** want them to (when I have that *It's all about me* attitude). After all, if I were in control, everything would work out perfectly and I would be in eternal bliss. But you and I both know this doesn't even come close to resembling reality.

So, what can we do about it? When it comes to control, we have only two choices:

1. We can attempt to take control or;
2. We can relinquish control.

Let's look at what happens when we choose to take control and how we can shift to relinquishing control.

## Give Me the Remote

Men are notorious for wanting the TV remote control, you know, "the clicker." We want control. We feel important when we have control. We can skip commercials. We can change channels in the middle of a show just to see what else is on...or just to annoy our wives. It's good to be king!

Wanting control is very normal. Control is one way we try to create our own security. This desire for control is not a new phenomenon. Citizens in Old Testament days built walls around their cities thinking this would provide security. President Reagan during the Cold War introduced a very controversial idea that was labeled "Star Wars." It was his strategic defense initiative that would protect America from enemy missiles. They would be shot down in space before they hit American soil. Again, creating security.

Our country still builds up our military defenses. Some people live in gated communities or with alarms on their doors and windows. Many build up their retirement accounts. All with the intent of taking control of security.

Before you go Rambo on me, I am not saying all this is bad. However, if you are like me, you may tend to take this control thing a bit overboard, which causes all sorts of stress. To take it a step further, when we try to control things, most times, if not all, we are doing so from a position of fear. Ultimately, we are saying that we need to control it because we are afraid that no one else, not even God, can help us. We think this way because we are focused on our lives, and therein lay the problem...our "alive" lives. Galatians 2:20a tells us this: *I have been crucified with Christ and I no longer live, but Christ lives in me.* To give up our desire to control, we must become dead to ourselves. A dead man can't worry or be anxious.

I have observed this in people I know who have faced major difficulties in their lives. Some of them acted as if their lives were over. They fretted and complained about the horrible hand that was dealt them. They were hyper-focused on what was happening TO them, which kept them stuck in the muck and mire.

On the other hand, I've observed others who seemed to be blessed in the midst of their difficult circumstances and in many cases, their tough situations proved to be the catalyst for something great in their lives. The one thing in common with each of the people in this group was that, at some point along the way, their thinking changed. **They shifted from thoughts of** *Why is this happening TO me?* **to** *What is God doing FOR me?* They each recognized that God was working on their behalf, even though in the natural it didn't seem like it at all. They became dead to themselves in their circumstances. Some of these, probably the more spiritually mature, went to this place quickly in the midst of their trial. Others may have taken a bit longer. But, they each got there and God was able to turn their lemons into lemonade.

A perfect example of this occurred in my life during the 18 months beginning in April, 2002. I was happily employed at a wonderful company in my area. The family that owned the business had sold it to a publicly traded company three years prior and our parent company had just brought in a new president to run our division. He and I hit it off right away and he asked me to be his Vice-President of Sales. I told him I wasn't interested because I had a pretty good thing going with my sales position and was quite content.

After several months of arm-twisting, I finally relented and took the VP position. Soon thereafter, I realized that I was going to be in for a long haul. My boss turned out to be the most tyrannical leader I have ever seen. It appeared that he believed in the adage that "The beatings will continue until morale improves." It became the most unhealthy work environment I could ever imagine.

For a year and a half, I found myself driving to the office in the morning with this gnawing pit in my stomach, just dreading to walk through the door of my office. I wondered what I was doing. I felt as if I was selling my soul for a paycheck. I was tired, stressed, and at times, very irritable. I oftentimes felt as if a Mack truck had just hit me. I was like a zombie.

My work situation spilled over into the other areas of my life. My wife and children desperately wanted me to get a new job so that their "normal" husband and daddy could come back. I was miserable and I was making those around me miserable as well. I look back on this and I can honestly say this was the most horrific time in my professional career. At the time, it was truly excruciating.

As you can see, I handled that situation very poorly. I chose to be angry when my boss "spit on me." I was clearly focused on my pain rather than on God. Sure, I was praying. Yes, I grew closer to the Lord during this season. However, had I truly been focused on my Father and had true faith in Him, I would have behaved much differently. I would have been having a conversation with God something like this: "Lord, thank you for this situation you have placed me in. I know you have me here for a reason. What are you trying to teach me? Please show me Lord and help me to respond appropriately." And, I certainly would have had more peace.

Though this was one of the most painful periods in my life and though I didn't handle it very well, I can now tell you that it was also one of the greatest moments in my life and is something for which I am incredibly thankful. Not only did God teach me in that season, but these circumstances led me to write my first book, *Bleedership, Biblical First-Aid for Leaders* in which I contrast the leadership style of my boss with that of some of the Bible's greatest leaders. Writing that book changed the entire trajectory of my life. I currently feel like the most blessed person on the earth that I get to do what I do. And none of it would have been possible had it not been for the "terrible" experience I had to go through.

I can't tell you when it happened for me but there was a point in time in which I went from hating my situation at work to actually being thankful for it. In other words, I eventually made the shift from complaining about what was happening TO me to praising God for what He was doing FOR me. In this case, I died to myself and I began to focus on Jesus.

## The Storms Of Life

As I write this chapter, it is late February. I am looking out the window of my home office and the scene is quite breathtaking. It seems that every tree branch in sight is glistening because of last night's ice storm. To my left is one of the several birch trees in our yard. It is approximately 30 feet tall and quite beautiful. Currently the top of the tree is resting on the ground, yet the tree is not broken...it looks like a big catapult.

Earlier today, I ran a quick errand and I noticed the wreckage all around our community. Many, many trees were destroyed from the weight of the ice. I saw some in which every branch of the tree was broken off and the only thing left was a short, stubby and lonely trunk. Many yards had branches littered about. Even some streets were temporarily closed because of the limbs in the road.

This left me wondering why some trees, like our birches, seemed to have survived the storm while others were killed or permanently scarred. I have noticed over the years that birch trees are very flexible. They sway with the wind and the storms. Other trees tend to be much more rigid and inflexible. It is those rigid trees whose branches were broken off in this storm. The birch and other flexible trees simply bent with the storm and will eventually return to their original condition, stronger for the experience.

The same is true in your life. If you are rigid and desirous of control, you, too, might have branches broken off which can leave painful scars, or worse. However, if you let go of your desire to control and let God have His way in your life, you can also be restored, a stronger person for the experience. Remember, God is working on your behalf. In **all** things, He is working FOR you (see Romans 8:28).

A lack of peace may occur in your heart when you try to take control of something in which you do not have control. This often happens because of the underlying fear that you may have in your heart...a fear that God is not going to provide or protect. This fear can then lead to worry and anxiety.

## Worry and Anxiety = Sin

This might surprise you, but worry and anxiety (or a lack of peace) is sin. It dishonors God, because when we worry or have anxiety in our hearts, we are effectively saying that God is not big enough to handle it, or that we trust ourselves more than we trust God. We are putting ourselves and our issues ahead of our Creator, which is the ultimate in pride and selfishness.

I have heard some argue that worry and anxiety are not considered sin because of what is commanded in 1 Peter 5:7: *Cast all your anxiety on him because he cares for you.* The argument is that we are expected to have anxiety in order to cast it on Him. However,

Romans 14:23 tells us that *everything that does not come from faith is sin*. Worry clearly does not come from faith, which means it is sin.

Because I have a natural bent to worry, I have a tendency to think of myself as having a long way to go in my Christian walk. Sometimes I feel like I have very little faith because of how stressed I feel about something. The reason I feel this way is that in those moments I am choosing to sin.

I read something that gave me great relief. Paul, who authored the majority of the New Testament, was obviously a godly man after his conversion. But, he still had issues just as you and I do. Check out what he wrote:

> Therefore I am all the more eager to send him, so that when you see him again you may be glad and *I may have less anxiety*. (Philippians 2:28, emphasis added)

Paul is talking about a guy named Epaphroditus. Paul stated that he will have less anxiety when Epaphroditus returns. So even the great Apostle Paul had anxiety. That helped me to realize that I am not alone in this struggle.

God knows all of our thoughts, even the anxious ones and He loves us anyway. With that being said, worry and anxiety are still sin and we need to stop. Worry can bind us from hearing the truth. In the parable of the sower, Jesus tells us what happens to the Word of God (the seed) when worry gets in the way:

> "The one who received the seed that fell among the thorns is the man who hears the word, but the worries of this life and the deceitfulness of wealth choke it, making it unfruitful." (Matthew 13:22)

Furthermore, Jesus tells of the dangers of anxiety in Luke 21:34:

> "Be careful, or your hearts will be weighed down with dissipation, drunkenness and the anxieties of life, and that

day will close on you unexpectedly like a trap."

Anxiety will cause our hearts to be weighed down. So why is that such a big deal? Well, what's one of the first things a medical professional does when he finds someone unconscious? He checks their pulse. He wants to see if their heart is still beating. The heart is the source of life and when it stops beating, we die. Our hearts are important! Check out what two different versions of Proverbs 4:23 have to say about our hearts:

> Above all else, guard your heart, for it is the wellspring of life. (NIV)
> Keep vigilant watch over your heart; *that's* where life starts. (Message)[1]

So, allowing our hearts to be weighed down with anxiety is very dangerous. When our hearts are right, we will be much less likely to give up our peace. Our hearts are where life begins. So we must do as Solomon instructed and guard, or keep vigilant watch over, our hearts.

As a reminder, we are to cast all our anxiety on Him (see 1 Peter 5:7). The verse that immediately follows gives us a warning about our enemy which should give us great pause on this subject:

> Be self-controlled and alert. Your enemy the devil prowls around like a roaring lion looking for someone to devour. (1 Peter 5:8)

## What about Spiritual Warfare?

"There are two equal and opposite errors into which our race can fall about the devils. One is to disbelieve in their existence. The other is to believe, and to feel an excessive and unhealthy interest in them. They themselves are equally pleased by both errors, and hail a materialist or magician with the same delight."[2]

C.S. Lewis from *The Screwtape Letters*

As we will discuss in coming chapters, God is a God of peace. God wants us to be in constant communion with Him and to have total peace in our hearts. However, I would be remiss if I didn't mention spiritual warfare. As C.S. Lewis stated above, it is an error to think that we do not have an enemy. It is just as equal an error to think that our enemy is around every tree.

The fact is, our enemy, Satan, is real and he will do all he can to keep us from God and His plans for our lives. Satan wants us to choose to give up our peace simply because God wants peace for us. His primary plan is to steal and kill and destroy (see John 10:10).

The first half of Matthew 4 reveals the temptations Jesus faced from Satan and how He dealt with them. This turns out to be a tremendous model for us in dealing with spiritual warfare and three things stick out to me. One, because Jesus was sinless, Satan had no power over Him. Two, Jesus knew the Word of God and used it as a weapon to combat Satan (as described in Ephesians 6:17 - the Sword of the Spirit). And three, the peace that Jesus exhibited in the midst of the warfare helped to defeat His adversary. Romans 16:20a says, *The God of peace will soon crush Satan under your feet.*

Not only are these great things to learn from but they will also be very important to remember in our quest for peace and will be discussed further in the coming pages.

While spiritual warfare is real and something we should be aware of, I believe that many of us get too wrapped up in it. I once heard a very famous motivational speaker at a conference talking about the time he visited a NASCAR racetrack and was given the opportunity to drive one of the cars around the track. As he was driving at well over 100 miles per hour, he could not help but regularly glance at the wall, which seemed to be only inches away from his fender. His coach who was monitoring his position on the racetrack firmly reminded him through his headphones, "Keep your eyes straight ahead! Don't focus on the wall!" The reason? Because each time he focused on the wall, he drifted closer and closer to it. Because of the crew chief's experience, he knew that if this rookie driver continued to look at the wall, he would eventually crash into it.

It was good that he knew there was a wall there and that it would be dangerous for him to run into it. However, he discovered that he shouldn't focus all his attention on it or that was where he was going to end up.

The same holds true for our enemy. It is good to know that he is real and he wants to separate us from God and from the peace He provides for us. However, just like the wall, we should not focus all our attention on our enemy. Our God is much bigger than him, so we should remain focused on God.

> Let us fix our eyes on Jesus, the author and perfecter of our faith, who for the joy set before him endured the cross, scorning its shame, and sat down at the right hand of the throne of God. (Hebrews 12:2)

**Takeaway:**
*Peace isn't stolen from us—we choose to give it up when we refuse to give up control or when we take our eyes off Jesus.*

## Prayer

Heavenly Father, You are amazing! Thank You for being You, the One in control! Lord, I want peace, the peace that can only come from You. Please forgive me for allowing worry, anxiety and circumstances to steal my peace. I know that this is really a control issue on my part. So please God help me guard my heart and protect me from the enemy and help me let go of those things I want to hang on to. Help me continue to recognize You as the One in control of everything. Amen.

# FOUR

# The Path to Peace

*"Peace be with you!"*
*John 20:19b*

*"Peace is not merely a distant goal that we seek,*
*but a means by which we arrive at the goal."*
*Martin Luther King*

Awise old man retired and purchased a modest home near a junior high school. He spent the first few weeks of his retirement in peace and contentment...then a new school year began. The next afternoon three young boys, full of youthful, after-school enthusiasm, came down his street, beating merrily on every trash can they encountered. The crashing percussion continued day after day, until finally the wise old man decided it was time to take some action.

The next afternoon, he walked out to meet the young percussionists as they banged their way down the street. Stopping them, he said, "You kids are a lot of fun. I like to see you express your exuberance like that. I used to do the same thing when I was your age. Will you do me a favor? I'll give you each a dollar if you'll promise to come around every day and do your thing."

The kids were elated and continued to do a bang-up job on the trash cans. After a few days, the old-timer greeted the kids again, but this time he had a sad smile on his face. "This recession's really putting a big dent in my income," he told them. "From now on, I'll only be able to pay you 50 cents to beat on the cans." The noisemakers were obviously displeased, but they did accept his offer and continued their afternoon ruckus.

A few days later, the wily retiree approached them again as they drummed their way down the street. "Look," he said, "I haven't received my Social Security check yet, so I'm not going to be able to give you more than 25 cents. Will that be okay?"

"A lousy quarter?" the drum leader exclaimed. "If you think we're going to waste our time, beating these cans around for a quarter, you're nuts! No way, mister. We quit!" And the old man enjoyed peace and serenity for the rest of his days.

This story makes me smile. It also shows me some incredible wisdom in action. This man knew what he was doing in order to establish peace in his neighborhood. He also knew it was going to be a process and he was patient. All things we can learn from. However, unlike this man, we don't have to bargain to get peace. It is readily available to each of us.

## A False Start I Am Thankful For

About four or five years ago, I began to write down some ideas about this book. In my mind it was going to look nothing like it does now. However, before going too far, I stopped. I just didn't feel like the book had any structure to it and because this was a huge project—I could have found myself chasing many rabbit trails.

About three years later, I began to be stirred again and felt that I was to begin writing once more but I still didn't have a framework for the book. So I began to ask God for help. I told Him that if He wanted me to write this He would need to give me something that would make sense to others.

I began to sense that God wanted me to use several verses in Philippians 4 as the primary framework for this project. Once again, I began laying out a few things but something still didn't seem right. Deep in my heart, I didn't want this to just be another book that people, after reading, would say, "That's nice," and put it on their shelf. I wanted it to be something that would actually drive people toward Christ and toward peace. I was looking for something that would help people to remember the truth of God's Word.

The Psalmist wrote, "I have hidden your word in my heart that I might not sin against you" (Psalm 119:11). Well, that is exactly what I wanted for this book: a tool that could help you hide God's Word in your heart, keeping you from worry and anxiety.

I wish I could tell you that some bright light appeared and a scroll was dropped from the sky with a revelation on it but I cannot. However, I did receive revelation. I can't explain it, but I just received a picture of a house in my head with an acronym that summarizes the basic framework for peace outlined in Philippians 4. God had answered my prayer and gave me the direction I needed to begin!

The peace that I have been seeking is the peace that Paul discusses in Philippians 4, *the peace that transcends all understanding*. I thought it would be a good idea to look a little deeper into this chapter to see if Paul reveals any keys to this doorway to peace, the peace that is beyond our comprehension.

Though written from a prison cell, Philippians has been called by many *Paul's joy letter* because the concept of *rejoicing* or *joy* appears sixteen times in the book's four chapters. In the midst of this joy letter, in just six short verses are some incredible keys that can help us unlock the door to peace. Here they are:

> Rejoice in the Lord always. I will say it again: Rejoice! Let your gentleness be evident to all. The Lord is near. Do not be anxious about anything, but in everything, by prayer and petition, with thanksgiving, present your requests to God. And the peace of God, which transcends all understanding, will guard your hearts and your minds in Christ Jesus.
>
> Finally, brothers, whatever is true, whatever is noble, whatever is right, whatever is pure, whatever is lovely, whatever is admirable—if anything is excellent or praiseworthy—think about such things. Whatever you have learned or received or heard from me, or seen in me—put it into practice. And the God of peace will be with you. (Philippians 4:4-9)

Looking at the last verse above, verse 9, Paul says, "Whatever you have learned or received or heard from me, or seen in me—put it into practice. And the God of peace will be with you." I don't know about you, but that sort of statement piques my interest. It makes me say, "Remind me again, what have you taught me? What have I heard you say? What have I seen you do?" Paul said that if we put these things into practice, we are promised that the God of peace will be with us. I want the God of peace with me—that is why I researched what Paul taught, said and did.

This also led me to think about something from my college basketball days at The University of Toledo. My coach, Bob Nichols who is now retired, was an incredible tactician who is extremely well respected in the college ranks. In fact, as of this writing, he has more wins than any men's coach in Mid-American Conference history. He knew the game and he knew how to get us into the right position. As a result, we won many games, though we weren't as physically gifted as many of our opponents.

During time-outs, we would be huddled around Coach Nichols as he gave us our instructions. It might have sounded something like this, "Okay, we need to do a better job of rebounding (looking right at me for some reason). We can't let them beat us down the court (again gazing at me, but I'm not sure why)! I want five passes before a shot." Then as we break and head for the court, he might say, "Zone defense on made shots and man-to-man on missed shots." The most important thing, or at least the thing he most wanted us to remember, was the last thing he told us, which in this case was the type of defense we would be playing.

As parents, we do the same thing with our kids...when they are headed to school, "Make sure you are polite to everyone," or when they are leaving for camp, "Don't forget to shower!"

I have to believe that Paul, in the verses above, is doing the same thing with us. "Whatever you have learned or received or heard from me, or seen in me—put it into practice. And the God of peace will be with you." So using this *last thing is most important* theory, we should look especially close at the things Paul shared just prior to verse nine. That is exactly what I set out to do as I tried to outline a framework for peace in our lives.

After many enhancements over the next year, I felt the book was complete. Several trusted people who had committed to read each new version agreed with my assessment and said it was ready to go to the publisher. Then came the feedback from Bob, one of my closest friends, whom I mentioned earlier. On the day before Easter, he and I met for breakfast to review the latest version of my manuscript. He said he liked many of the changes, but some of the major parts of the book, in particular the "house of peace" I described, just didn't make sense to him and he thought it seemed "contrived." Normally when hearing something like this I would have been defensive or dismissive all for the sake of completing the project (especially when the majority were saying it was ready).

However, when he shared this with me, all I can say was that this agreed with me and I had total peace about what he was saying. Deep down, I knew some major changes needed to be made. So, this "house of peace" got blown up, torn down, leveled...and I was actually excited about what God might have in store despite the fact that I was going to have to go back to the drawing board. So that day I began to ask God what He wanted me to do with this. (If you'd like to see what this House of Peace looked like, you can go to Appendix E at calmingthestormwithin.com/appendix).

The very next day, Easter morning, I was asked to give the announcements at our church, meaning I would be at all three of our services. I attended the first service with my family. After my announcement time at the second service, I retreated to my pastor's office to spend some quiet time with God. During that time, something amazing happened. I began reading in John 14 and I felt like I was given new eyes because I was looking at this section of Scripture in a completely new light. As I read on, I discovered that Jesus' teaching in John 14-16 lined up almost exactly with the verses from Philippians and even shed additional light on a game plan for finding peace. This was clear confirmation to me that God did have something else in store for this book. I was fired up to say the least and was in awe that the God of the universe would speak to me in such a personal way!

## Paul's Way to Peace

Let's revisit Paul's instructions again:

> Rejoice in the Lord always. I will say it again: Rejoice! Let your gentleness be evident to all. The Lord is near. Do not be anxious about anything, but in everything, by prayer and petition, with thanksgiving, present your requests to God. And the peace of God, which transcends all understanding, will guard your hearts and your minds in Christ Jesus.

Finally, brothers, whatever is true, whatever is noble, whatever is right, whatever is pure, whatever is lovely, whatever is admirable—if anything is excellent or praiseworthy—think about such things. Whatever you have learned or received or heard from me, or seen in me—put it into practice. And the God of peace will be with you. (Philippians 4:4-9)

In the verses above, Paul is telling us the following:
- Rejoice always...regardless of your circumstances;
- Be gentle—some translations say "considerate"—with others;
- Know that God is always with you or nearby (Some scholars think this could also mean that we are to let our gentleness be known because the Lord is coming back soon.);
- Choose not to be anxious;
- Go to God in prayer, with thanksgiving, for everything...even small stuff;
- Keep your mind focused on good things...in other words, "garbage in, garbage out."

Paul further states that if we can do these things, the God of peace will be with us. The shorter version of this might read, *Pray right, think right and live right and you will have peace which cannot be explained.* While I am not a huge fan of "5 steps to _____ (fill in the blank)," Paul was clearly onto something very important when he penned Philippians 4. He was given instructions, which he passed onto us on how to find the peace, which transcends all understanding. On the surface, doing any one of these things might seem easy to you. You might be successful at times with not being anxious or being joyful when things are going sideways, but the fact is that this is not sustainable unless you have some help. None of us can do this on our own.

A logical question would be, *Why would Paul give the Philippians (and us) steps to follow which, on the surface, appear impossible?* That is a great question. However, these steps aren't impossible. We can do them, but again, only if we have help. The good news is that Jesus clearly outlines how we can tap into this help and turn the impossible into the possible...and truly experience the peace, which transcends all understanding.

## The Master Plan

In John, chapter 13 we get a glimpse into what occurred during The Last Supper, the night before Jesus was to be crucified. We are shown how Jesus modeled servant leadership by washing the feet of His disciples; even the feet of Judas whom He knew would betray Him. Then we see how Jesus predicted His betrayal and that Judas fled. Finally, we are shown that Jesus predicted Peter's denial of Him.

Jesus had just shared some heavy stuff with his closest followers. I'm sure they had to be thinking that something big was going down. Suffice it to say, He surely had their attention. **So the words Jesus spoke next must be pretty important.** These would be the last words Jesus would share with his disciples before His arrest and they give us clear instructions, which tie directly to the level of peace He wants you and me to have. The following is a brief outline of those teachings from John 14-16:

1) Do not let your hearts be troubled (or don't be anxious)...14:1, 27b;
2) Here's why you don't need to be anxious...14:2-3, 28-31;
3) Here's the only way to go...14:4-14;
4) Be obedient...14:15, 15:14;
5) Jesus will then send a Helper...14:16-26; 16:5-15;
6) Then Jesus will leave you with peace...14:27a;
7) Intimacy with Jesus is key...15:1-17;
8) This intimacy with Jesus will lead to:
   a) Your joy being complete...15:11;
   b) A greater level of love...15:12-13;
   c) God's words in you...15:7;
   d) A more effective prayer life...14:14; 15:7,16; 16:23;

9) Jesus gives you warnings of what to look out for...15:18-16:4; 16:16-28;

10) He then lets the disciples know that despite His warnings, they would not listen and they would not have peace (and this is very instructive to us as we will see later)...16:31-32;

11) Jesus reminds us of how we can have peace...16:33.

Paul's instructions in Philippians are excellent and very practical. However, if we haven't followed the teaching of Jesus in John 14-16, it will be for naught. In pursuing peace, we must be mindful of both the teachings of Paul and the teachings of Jesus. The last recorded words of Jesus to His disciples prior to His arrest are these:

> "I have told you these things, so that in me *you may have peace*. In this world you will have trouble. But take heart! I have overcome the world." (John 16:33, emphasis added)

Peace for us is obviously something that is important to Jesus. We will now be looking more closely at the things He shared so that we may have peace.

 **Takeaway:** *The concept of inner peace does not have to be a pipe dream. It is possible and it is something God desires for us...and He has given us a path to follow to peace.*

## Prayer

Lord God, I am so thankful that You have provided a way to peace. You know my heart Lord, and you know that I desire peace. Please open my eyes to see and my heart to understand as I read the coming pages. Show me a new way Father. Please don't let me be deceived. I'm counting on You. I'm trusting You. God, lead me. Amen.

# The Master's Plan

As mentioned in the previous chapter, Paul gives some very clear instructions on how we can find peace in our lives. However, these instructions are impossible to follow on our own. We need help. Jesus tells us about the help we all need and provides us with clear direction which will directly impact the level of peace each of us experiences. The coming section will explore His teaching and will provide light for our path.

Here is what we will explore in the coming chapters...

# The Only Way

*Jesus answered, "I am the way and the truth and the life.*
*No one comes to the Father except through me."*
*John 14:6*

*"No God, no peace. Know God, know peace."*
*Unknown*

Jesus said, "I am the way and the truth and the life. No one comes to the Father except through me" (John 14:6). Controversial words to say the least. Jesus is saying there is only one way. One way to the Father. One way to eternal life. One way to life to the full, including peace. On the surface this sounds awfully exclusive. However, it is actually radically *inclusive* because the door is open to everyone:

- Regardless of your race;
- Regardless of your religious upbringing;
- Regardless of what you have done in your past—Jesus promises to wipe the slate clean...for real!

However, according to Jesus, "...wide is the gate and broad is the road that leads to destruction, and many enter through it. But small is the gate and narrow the road that leads to life, and only a few find it." (Matthew 7:13b-14) So unfortunately, though Jesus' invitation is available to all, few will accept it.

Too many of us live life thinking like the unknown author of this poem:

> God grant that I may live to fish until my dying day
> And when my final cast is made
> And life has slipped away,
> I pray that God's great landing net
> Will catch me in its sweep
> And in His mercy, God will judge me
> Big enough to keep.

*And in His mercy, God will judge me big enough to keep.* That is how many people feel about God and what it takes to enter the kingdom of Heaven...if we are "big" enough for God to keep. Unfortunately, that is how I felt for much of my life...that if I did enough good things to outweigh the bad things, then God would let me into Heaven.

It is said that on occasion Oliver Wendell Holmes, the famous author, would get on a train to journey across the country with no real destination in mind. On one such trip, shortly after departing the station, the conductor came through the train to collect the tickets. When he came to Holmes, Holmes could not find his ticket. He searched everywhere to no avail. The conductor recognized him and said, "That's alright Mr. Holmes. Don't worry about it. I'm sure you wouldn't have gotten on this train if you hadn't bought a ticket. You can just mail it in when you get home."

"Young man," Holmes said, "that's not my problem. I'm not concerned about you getting your ticket; I just want to know where I'm going!"

There was only one difference between Holmes and me. He *knew* he was lost while I thought I had it all figured out. But Heaven wasn't a certainty for me—I didn't think it could be. I kind of thought I was going to go to Heaven but I wasn't really sure. In truth, I didn't know where I was going. I was lost.

To give you some background, I grew up in a great family and was taught many good values. I was even taken to church every now and then (occasionally on Christmas and Easter). And I hated every minute of it. I was completely bored and saw it as a complete waste of time.

After I got married and we began to have children, Connie and I decided that it made sense to begin attending church, as it would be good for our kids. So we did and we really started to enjoy it. Both of us began volunteering in different areas and felt as if we were doing great stuff for God.

During that time I found myself searching for peace and relaxation. You see, I was raised to believe that true security could only come from having a bunch of money in the bank. As a result, I worked hard and strived to save as much money as I could because I really wanted that security, or peace.

My success was defined by my income and my net worth. The funny thing about this is that as my income and net worth began to grow, my level of peace seemed to decrease. My stress level was going up as my income rose. That was not supposed to happen.

Then in 1999, a good friend suggested that I read the book, *Left Behind*.[1] This was the first of a 12-book series that was just being released at the time. The fictional series takes a look at what the end times might look like based on the author's view (a pre-tribulation, futurist viewpoint) of the book of Revelation, the last book in the Bible.

Early in the book, I was introduced to one of the main characters, Rayford Steele, who is an airline pilot. I discovered that he was contemplating having an affair with one of his flight attendants and that he was disgusted with his wife who was always reading her Bible and praying. He was tired of her asking him to go to church with her.

During the flight, his panicked flight attendant came into the cockpit to declare that many of the passengers on the plane were missing. Rayford didn't believe it so he went to check it out only to find that it was true. Many seats were empty except for the clothing, jewelry, and books that lay there.

Rayford then learned that this was happening all over the world. Planes were crashing because pilots were missing. *Chaos* was the word of the day.

As quickly as he could, Rayford landed his plane back in his hometown of Chicago. He rushed home to find that his wife and son were both missing. Their pajamas were neatly in their beds under the covers.

Later, Rayford's older daughter rushed in wanting to know what had happened. Out of ideas, they headed for the church (that Rayford's wife and son regularly attended) and found the associate pastor there. The pastor explained that Jesus had returned to "rapture" His church. He went on to say that all those who had placed their faith in Him were taken up to Heaven with Jesus and the rest were left behind. Rayford then said something like this: "If this is true, why are you still here? You're a pastor!"

The pastor explained that he now knew that he didn't have a personal relationship with Jesus and had never invited Him in to be the ruler of his life. He said he was just going through the motions and "doing" lots of good things. He thought that was what it was all about.

At that point it hit me. That was me! I was in the same boat as that pastor. I was doing good things, but I hadn't put my faith in Jesus. I hadn't acknowledged Him as the leader of my life and I hadn't committed to follow Him. So right then and there I made that decision and commitment.

I then began—I admit, it was slow at first—to seek after and to follow Jesus. In doing so, I discovered a level of peace I had not known before. I would love to tell you that from that point forward, I had no more fear, anxiety or worries, but that just isn't true. It has been a process that is still ongoing. I'm not where I want to be, but thank God I'm not where I used to be!

Looking back over my life, it was chaos, which led me to Jesus. Almost everyone I know who is a follower of Jesus came to Him in the midst of chaos or trouble in his or her lives. Unfortunately, prosperity seldom, if ever, draws us closer to Him.

## Substitutionary Atonement

I once heard Bill Hybels deliver a message in which he said, "The entire message of the Christian faith can be summarized by these two words, *Substitutionary Atonement.*"

Let's look at both of these words.

*Atonement* is "payment for an infraction" while *Substitutionary* means, "to take the place of." In other words, the Christian faith is all about our infractions being paid for by Someone Else. Christianity is the only religion in the world in which this is true. *All others preach self-atonement.*

In God's eyes, blood must be shed anytime sin occurs. In fact, the law requires that nearly everything be cleansed with blood, and without the shedding of blood there is no forgiveness (see Hebrews 9:22). So let's look at some Old Testament stories to show how this played out.

When Adam and Eve first sinned, God came down and killed an animal to provide clothing. Blood was shed and it was shed by an innocent third party, in this case, an animal (see Genesis 3:21).

God once told the Jews to kill their prize lamb and spread the blood from the lamb on their doorways so that He would know to "pass over" their house and not kill the first-born son and animal. Blood was shed because of sin, again, from an innocent third party (see Exodus 12).

In Leviticus 16 we learn of the Day of Atonement. It was on this day that the community would gather around the high priest and two goats. One of the goats was killed, the shedding of blood by another innocent third party. The high priest would then metaphorically transfer the sins of all the people to the second goat. Then the goat would be sent to the wilderness to die signifying that their sins had been atoned or paid for. (This is where we get the term "scapegoat" by the way.)

Then in the New Testament, in John 1:29, we see John the Baptist say, "Look, the Lamb of God, who takes away the sin of the world!" In other words, John was saying, "Look, here comes our scapegoat!"

Fast-forward to the cross. Just as Jesus breathed His last, He said, "It is finished" (John 19:30). Jesus didn't say this because He was giving up. He was saying, "It's done. The atonement has been paid...for all mankind!"

So why do we need this atonement?

Romans 3:23 says that all of us have sinned and fallen short of the glory of God. Every single one of us. As a result, we are separated from God because He can't be in the presence of sin. He is a Holy God. Obviously, this is not good news for us, as we are all sinners.

As if this wasn't bad enough, Romans 6:23 tells us that the wages of sin is death. So what we are due, our paycheck so to speak, is death. Not just a physical death but an everlasting spiritual death completely separated from our Heavenly Father. Not pretty.

However, Romans 10:9 gives us hope: <u>If you confess with your mouth, "Jesus is Lord," and believe in your heart that God has raised Him from the dead then you will be saved.</u>

Here's the rub: what is being discussed in Romans 10:9 is the exact opposite of a wage. It is a gift. We cannot earn it. We can only choose to receive it or reject it.

When we choose to receive this gift from God, the gift that Jesus paid for us, this not only allows us to live with God in Heaven for eternity but He allows us to be fully alive, here and now (see John 10:10). He gives us a way to find peace with God, the peace that transcends all understanding.

I don't know about you, but I don't want anything to do with a wage of death (an eternal death). I want the gift that Jesus gave, which is eternal life and life to the full.

In Revelation 3:20 Jesus says, "Here I am! I stand at the door and knock. If anyone hears my voice and opens the door, I will come in and eat with him, and he with me." He stands at the door and knocks. He is a gentleman. He won't force His way in.

He's waiting for you. So you have a choice to make. You can choose to open the door and accept the gift that Jesus has for you or you can choose not to *which is actually rejecting Him.* Because God gave us free will, we all have a choice, each one of us. Either we will choose to accept Christ for who He is or we will choose to reject Him. There is no middle ground.

The tough part is this: choosing to accept Jesus as your Lord and Savior is not the easy path...at least not in this life on earth. This is not just a ticket to heaven, which allows you to continue with life as usual. No. It is my opinion that we mess this up in the Church. We tell people they can say a certain prayer and be "saved." (In fact, I don't see anywhere in the Bible where a "prayer" is necessary for salvation.) We focus on the "and you will be saved" part of Romans 10:9 but we forget the "Jesus is Lord" part of that same verse. If someone is your lord, you follow them and obey them. When we commit to this with Jesus, we are in essence committing to an exchange, our life for the life of Jesus.

If you make this commitment it will mean that you will have some scary moments; Jesus said so. It may make you feel extremely unsafe and unsure at times. You may face pain and heartache. You may be asked by Him to do things you don't want to do. But the good news is that a life lived through Him is guaranteed to be much richer, fuller and more meaningful than a life lived without Him. Though it may feel unsteady at times, being in His arms is truly the safest place you can be, and, it brings peace, which you never thought was possible.

If you have not made this commitment, I encourage you to do so now. Simply make your own commitment from your heart. Jesus knows your heart, so he'll know if you mean it. It could sound something like this:

> "Jesus, I need help and forgiveness. I can't save myself, only You can. Thank you for dying for me and for being my scapegoat. I want You to be my Lord. I commit from this day forward to serve You, to follow You, to obey You. Please show me the way to do all these things."

If you have not made this decision, would you stop reading right now and ask yourself what is stopping you? I'm very serious about this. Put the book down for at least a day and really ponder this question: *What is keeping me from following Jesus?* Write down all the reasons. Ask God to show you the way. Find a mature Christian who can talk through this with you.

I cannot stress this enough. This is critical not only for your eternal destination but also for the peace you experience on this earth. The fact is that until you make this decision, it will be impossible to find the peace that God desires for you. So again, please put the book down and come back to this spot when you have made that decision or at least a day has passed. I even put a mark on the page to show you where you left off...

------

If you have decided to welcome Jesus as your Lord and Savior, congratulations! Angels are rejoicing in heaven (see Luke 15:10) and your name is now written in the Lamb's Book of Life (see Revelation 20:15). You have a new identity. The Holy Spirit now resides inside of you and will give you the desire to glorify God. It is very important that you tell some others about your commitment—the verse I mentioned earlier said, "If you confess with your mouth..." So, it is important to say this out loud to someone. Tell someone you know who is a believer. This will really encourage them and they can help you to take the next steps.

Keep in mind that this is not something to take lightly. You have made a commitment to the Creator of the Universe that Jesus is your new Lord, your CEO, your Boss. Anytime you get a new boss, you want to find out what he wants you to do, right? No different here. You will want to find out how to walk with Him and follow Him.

You were not meant to go on this journey alone. You were meant to travel with others.

Ecclesiastes 4:9-10 says, *Two are better than one, because they have a good return for their work: If one falls down, his friend can help him up. But pity the man who falls and has no one to help him up!* The fact is that others can help you when you stumble. They can also challenge you, hold you accountable and help you to grow as Proverbs 27:17 teaches us: *As iron sharpens iron, so one man sharpens another.* This is extremely important—don't try to do this alone! I encourage you to find a group or at least one person who can help you in this way.

I also challenge you to ask around and do some research to find a Bible-believing, Kingdom-minded church or group of people. Then find someone to teach you how to read the Bible and develop an intimate relationship with God. Again, ask. Don't worry about feeling awkward. Everyone has been in the same spot as you are in now. In fact, I think you'll find most Christians excited for you and eager to help.

Begin to pray about everything. Talk with God; He is your friend, so talk with Him that way. We will discuss this further in Chapter 12.

## Saved From or Saved To?

I want to share another thing I believe we get wrong way too often. More often than not, we, as Christians, focus too much on the process of salvation as being something that we are being saved *from*. It is true that once you are saved you are no longer destined for Hell. However, I like to look at this as something we are being saved *to*. Not only are we saved to an eternal life in heaven with God, but we are also saved so that we can experience life to the full...right here and right now (see John 10:10).

I see very few Christians living "life to the full." Perhaps the biggest reason for this goes back to something that we covered earlier...control. Most people want Jesus and the promise of heaven, but they don't want to give up control of their lives. They want to treat Him like they do a breakfast buffet, taking only what they want and leaving the "unappetizing" things. As a result, they miss out on one of the greatest gifts Jesus has for them: a full life, including peace. Much of this desire to control is caused when we dwell on the past or worry about the future.

## Living in the Moment

You might be saying, "Jim, you talk about peace like it's so easy to find. You don't understand my circumstances. Things are really tough right now and I just can't get away from this anxiety."

Believe me, I do understand. I may not totally get your circumstances and what you are specifically going through, but I do understand the anxiety part. I have probably been one of God's biggest projects when it comes to overcoming anxiousness.

Regardless of what is going on in your life, you must know God's stance on this. First of all, He knows we are going to have trouble in our lives, in fact, Jesus promised it to us:

"In this world you will have trouble." (John 16:33b)

Sounds pretty ominous, doesn't it? Why would Jesus promise us something like this? Well, let's look at this verse in its entirety:

"I have told you these things, so that *in me you may have peace. In this world you will have trouble. But take heart! I have overcome the world*" (emphasis added).

So, yes, we will have trouble. But Jesus has overcome all that! He came so that in Him we may have peace. That is what God wants for us...peace! In fact, He has already given it to us:

> But the fruit of the Spirit is love, joy, peace, patience, kindness, goodness, faithfulness, gentleness and self-control. (Galatians 5:22-23a)

As mentioned, when we trust Jesus as our Savior, we receive the Holy Spirit. The nine fruit of the Holy Spirit listed above include peace. Just like an orange tree will produce oranges, the Spirit in us will produce peace if we open ourselves to this.

Unfortunately, many of us live and show the fruit of our circumstances. But we are to exhibit the fruit of the Spirit, and not just when things are going great in our lives. This is to be something that we show at all times, with the Spirit's help. What I have found to be true is that, much like working out, the more we exercise our "fruit," the easier it becomes to exhibit it. So how do we do that?

Over the course of my life, I have had a tendency to compound my troubles by adding to them the *possibility* of trouble. I would not only try to deal with my current troubles but I would also try to deal with future troubles that might not ever come. This is called worry.

Jesus did promise trouble, but He didn't ask us to take on the trouble in our future. In fact, in Matthew 6:34, Jesus tells us, "Therefore do not worry about tomorrow, for tomorrow will worry about itself. *Each day has enough trouble of its own*" (emphasis added). Clearly, Jesus is instructing us to not be worrying about the future.

In *How to Stop Worrying and Start Living*, Dale Carnegie shares a story about Sir William Osler. As a medical student at Montreal General Hospital, Osler was worried about passing his final examination, where he was going to live and how he was going to build a practice and make a living. He picked up a book and read twenty words that had a radical impact on his future.

These words, from Thomas Carlyle, were, *"Our main business is not to see what lies dimly at a distance, but do what clearly lies at hand."*[2]

Forty-two years later, Osler, who was incredibly successful, addressed the graduating class of Yale University. He shared what he considered the secret of his success—living in "day-tight compartments."

A few months prior, Osler had crossed the Atlantic on an impressive ocean liner. On the voyage, he learned that the captain of the ship, with the push of a button, could shut off sections of the ship from each other, into watertight compartments.

He went on to tell the students that they were each much more amazing than this great ocean liner, but they needed to learn something from the impressive ship. They, also, needed to live within compartments. He exhorted the students to stand on the bridge of "their ship", shut off the past and the future, and focus only on what lies ahead of them at that moment.

He wasn't saying for them (and us) to not prepare for tomorrow. What he did say is that the best way to prepare for tomorrow is to focus on doing today's work with excellence. He further urged the students to begin the day with Christ's prayer, "Give us this day our daily bread." He said that Jesus didn't tell us to pray for yesterday's or tomorrow's bread, only today's. We must live in the moment.

If we spend too much time in the past, we can be filled with regret. If we spend too much time in the future, we can be filled with worry. Living in the moment allows us to truly set our minds on not being caught up in our circumstances. We can rejoice in the Lord always knowing that all things are going to work out for good for those who love God and are called according to His purpose (see Romans 8:28).

Living in the moment can not only help your level of peace, but think about some of the other improvements you might see in your:

· Listening skills;

- Clarity;
- Compassion for others;
- Role as a spouse;
- Role as a parent;
- Role as a friend;
- Ability to do your job effectively;
- Etc...

There are many benefits to living in the moment. When we get caught up in letting tomorrow take up too much of today, we are not living in the moment. We are letting go of our peace.

*Yesterday is history. Tomorrow is a mystery. Today is a gift—that's why they call it the present.* I love that statement but I never considered it Biblical until I considered that God refers to Himself as "I Am" throughout the Bible. There is a reason for this, as Helen Mallicoat shares:

# I AM

I was regretting the past and fearing the future.
Suddenly my Lord was speaking.
**"My name is I AM."**
He paused. I waited. He continued,
"When you live in the past with its mistakes and
regrets, it is hard. I am not there.
**My name is not I WAS.**
When you live in the future, with its problems and
fears, it is hard. I am not there.
**My name is not I WILL BE.**
When you live in this moment it is not hard.
I am here,
**My name is I AM."**

## God of Peace

The peace that God wants for us is not supposed to be something that only "super-Christians" are supposed to attain. It is for all of us:

The LORD gives strength to his people; the LORD blesses his people with peace. (Psalm 29:11)

Therefore, since we have been justified through faith, we have peace with God through our Lord Jesus Christ. (Romans 5:1)

"Peace I leave with you; my peace I give you. I do not give to you as the world gives. Do not let your hearts be troubled and do not be afraid." (John 14:27)

The peace that is described in the above verses cannot be obtained at a store, through a doctor or from a drug. It can only be received from God. Did you know that of all the adjectives that describe God, He is referred to in Scripture as the "God of peace" more than any other? (Judges 6:24, Isaiah 9:6, Romans 15:33 and 16:20, 1 Corinthians 14:33, Philippians 4:9, 1 Thessalonians 5:23, Hebrews 13:20, Ephesians 2:14). He desperately wants us to find peace, the peace that can only come from Him. And, the good news is that it is readily available to (and attainable for) all of us.

 **Takeaway:**
*God is the God of peace. The only way to the God of peace is through His Son, Jesus.*

## Prayer

Dear God, I am so thrilled and so thankful that You are the God of Peace. Thank you for sending Your Son to die for my sins and to make a way to You. I know that it is only through that sacrifice that peace is possible for me and for that I am so thankful. Lord, help me to live in the moment and help me to have life to the full. Thank you God! Amen.

# Intimacy

*"Remain in me, and I will remain in you.*
*No branch can bear fruit by itself; it must remain in the vine.*
*Neither can you bear fruit unless you remain in me."*
John 15:4

*"To fall in love with God is the greatest of all romances; To seek Him,*
*the greatest adventure; To find him, the greatest human achievement."*
*Augustine*

When someone asks you a question like this, "Do you know John Smith?", there are several possible responses, each showing a different level of relationship. Here are some:

1. Sure. I know who he is.
2. Sure. We went to high school together.
3. Sure. He and I are friends.
4. Sure. He and I see each other every week and we talk often.
5. Sure. He and I are best friends. We tell each other everything—nothing is a secret between us. We help each other become the person God designed us to be.

God wants a relationship with you like the one described in No. 5 above. He wants to be your best Friend. He wants intimacy with you.

This book is filled with Biblical principles, which, if followed, will bring peace to your life. However, in order to have true, everlasting peace, you must embrace and desire the presence...God's presence. It is only through intimacy with your Heavenly Father that you can experience the peace, which transcends all understanding.

Let me repeat that, **It is only through intimacy with your Heavenly Father that you can experience the peace, which transcends all understanding. You cannot experience the level of peace, which God makes available for you without knowing Him at a deep level. If you remember nothing else from this book, please hold onto this fact. I implore you to do everything you can to grow in your intimacy with Christ.**

I am not saying that Biblical principles are not good—they are. In fact, they are so powerful that they work for everyone, even those who don't believe in Jesus. The truth is, if a non-believer follows Biblical principles, his life will be enhanced.

But if you combine the application of the Biblical principles outlined in this book with an intimate relationship with God, you *will* experience peace that you did not think was possible, the peace which transcends all understanding.

My friend Bob has a great business mind. He usually has an answer for just about any issue someone might have in his or her business. He told me of a meeting he had with a friend of ours, a business owner who was struggling with some issues in his company. This owner had to make some decisions.

As he was talking, Bob was thinking to himself, "I just know he's going to ask me what I would do, but I don't have an answer." He said he began praying that God would give him something to say that would help our friend. In that moment, God whispered to him,

"No, you don't have an answer. But I want you to point him to the One who does have the answer."

That is the purpose of this book. I realize that I too, don't know all the answers. But I know the One who does and I want to point you toward Him.

## The Gardener

"I am the true vine, and my Father is the gardener. He cuts off every branch in me that bears no fruit, while every branch that does bear fruit he prunes so that it will be even more fruitful. You are already clean because of the word I have spoken to you. Remain in me, and I will remain in you. No branch can bear fruit by itself; it must remain in the vine. Neither can you bear fruit unless you remain in me.

"I am the vine; you are the branches. If a man remains in me and I in him, he will bear much fruit; apart from me you can do nothing. If anyone does not remain in me, he is like a branch that is thrown away and withers; such branches are picked up, thrown into the fire and burned. If you remain in me and my words remain in you, ask whatever you wish, and it will be given you. This is to my Father's glory, that you bear much fruit, showing yourselves to be my disciples." (John 15:1-8)

In the above verses, Jesus paints a picture we can all relate to, that of a vine or plant. We all know that if we cut a branch from the main trunk or vine, that branch will die and be of no use. Jesus uses this to tell us that He is the vine, we are the branches and God is the gardener with the lopping sheers.

We are to "remain" in Jesus so that we can "bear fruit." To remain in Him means that we are to stay connected. We are to continually seek Him. Jesus further states that "apart from me you can do nothing" (v. 5b). I have been coming to the realization that intimacy with God the Father and God the Son is the key to our spiritual journey. "Apart from Me you can do nothing." Nothing. Nada.

Zip. Without Jesus, we can do nothing...at least nothing of true value. **If you get nothing else out of this book, please get this: intimacy with Jesus is of paramount importance and the most important thing you can develop to help you find the peace, which transcends all understanding.** This is so important; I'm going to repeat it. **If you get nothing else out of this book, please get this: intimacy with Jesus is of paramount importance and the most important thing you can develop to help you find the peace, which transcends all understanding.**

So how is this intimacy created? It takes two, right? It does, but Jesus is sure to point out that if we are not enjoying intimacy with Him, it is not His fault...it's ours. "Remain in Me, ***and*** I will remain in you" (v. 15:4a, emphasis added). The "and" that Jesus uses here is relevant. It means that if we do our part, He will do His. It is up to us to move first, however.

## Developing Intimacy

The very first time I saw my wife, Connie, she was leading cheers on the sidelines for The University of Toledo's football team. I was instantly captivated by her and could not take my eyes off her. From that moment on, I did everything I could to be around her. I changed my normal patterns and routines so that I could be where she was going to be. When we began dating, I wanted to spend every minute I could with her. I wanted to know as much about her as possible.

God is longing for that same type of relationship with you. He desperately wants you to know Him better. It is through this intimate connection that He will do amazing things in you, including making peace available to you at a level you never thought possible.

As mentioned in the last chapter, when you become a follower of Jesus, you are given the Holy Spirit. Once you have the Holy Spirit, an automatic byproduct is the fruit of the Spirit as outlined in Galatians 5:22-23. One of the nine fruit listed is peace. So how do you bear that fruit? How does this become evident in your life?

Jesus gives us the answer when He tells us, "Remain in Me, and I will remain in you. No branch can bear fruit by itself; it must remain in the vine. *Neither can you bear fruit unless you remain in Me*" (John 15:4, emphasis added). Jesus is telling us that the only way to have this fruit become active in us is by remaining, or abiding, in Him. In order to find true peace we must abide in Him.

The only way to abide, or develop this intimacy with God, is the same way you did with your spouse (if you're married) when you were dating...through time with Him. You can't get drive-through or microwave intimacy. It just doesn't happen that way. It takes intentional time with Him. That time might look different for each of us, but it can include things such as worship, prayer, fasting, reading and studying His Word, journaling, listening for God's voice or meditating on His Word. A very wise friend of mine named Dan once observed, "You can be efficient with your stuff, but if you want to develop a solid relationship, you must be very inefficient in that relationship." In other words, you must be willing to spend time in that relationship. This certainly holds true in our relationship with God.

Jesus modeled this throughout the Gospels. We often see that He went off to be alone with His heavenly Father even when, and maybe especially when, His day was crazy busy. Luke 5:16 says, "But Jesus often withdrew to lonely places and prayed." In other places, it says that He simply withdrew to be by Himself (with God). He doesn't give us a checklist to follow other than prayer, but He does show that spending intentional time with God was important to Him, which means it should be important to us, too.

In my experience, spending time with God was not something I wanted to do. It was very unnatural for me. To be honest, the thought of it sounded quite weird to me. In fact, I recently took a personality profile that scored my personality in six areas. The two highest-ranking areas for me were very action oriented. My lowest ranked area was called "Dreamer" and was at 0%. The materials stated that a 0% was almost impossible, yet for this personality type who likes to spend quiet time alone, I was a zero. I share this to tell you that being alone and seeking God is truly not my default setting.

Despite all this, I wanted to know God more so I started getting up earlier in the morning to spend time with Him reading His Word. (I began by reading a chapter in Proverbs each day. Proverbs has 31 chapters, so I would read the chapter coinciding with the day of the month.) My intentional time with God has since increased over time, is ever changing and even includes occasional retreats where I spend large chunks of time just being in His presence.

Preparing for my first retreat was pretty comical. *What would I do during this time? Will anyone see me? What if God isn't there? What if I do something wrong? What if God doesn't hear me? Won't I be bored?* These were all questions that went through my head.

I began to realize that none of my concerns was valid and that God would accept me just as I am. I couldn't do anything wrong if I was seeking Him. There is no "formula." I could just "be" with Him. God says this in Jeremiah 29:13-14a: "You will seek me and find me, when you seek me with all your heart. I will be found by you." God knows your heart. He promises that if you are seeking Him with all your heart, you **will** find Him. He doesn't mention what you need to do, just that your heart is set on seeking Him.

If your heart is truly set on seeking God, your actions will soon follow. You will begin to choose to do some things differently. You may develop a hunger to learn techniques in studying the Bible or ways to journal or anything else that might take you into deeper fellowship with God. But the key in all of this is to have a heart set on seeking Him. You can pick these other things up along the way from spiritual leaders you know and from books. (If you would like some tools and ideas to help you in developing this intimacy with God, I invite you to go to calmingthestormwithin.com/intimacy.) Please remember though, there is no formula or 3-step program for this. This is between you and God.

What I have discovered is that the more time I spend with God, the more I hear from Him. (Jesus said in John 8:47, "He who belongs to God hears what God says. The reason you do not hear is that you do not belong to God.") Also, the more time I spend with Him the more I *want* to spend time with Him. I have found that when I do spend intentional time with God, things just seem to go more smoothly for me. I have definitely noticed an increased level of peace in my life and I have grown to love this time with Him. I now see it as the most productive thing I can do. Weird, perhaps...but true.

I share this with you not to impress you, but rather to encourage you. I may be one of the most "task-oriented", "get my stuff done" kind of guys I know. If *I* can slow down to do this, If *I* can have my thinking totally changed, if *I* can see that this is my most productive time, anyone can. The past two years have been an amazing time of growth for me with God. I feel closer to Him than ever. I truly know that I have a friend in Him and my faith in Him has increased considerably. All because I have chosen to seek after God.

If you are someone who thinks you cannot be intimate with God because of your schedule or because of where you work or for any other reason, check out this story. Denise, a very good family friend shared with me about a time she took a job in a business that she knew nothing about. Because of her lack of knowledge about the business, she often felt very anxious so she found herself running to the bathroom with regularity so she could be alone with God and ask Him for help. She said that the owners later told her that they thought she had some physical issues because she was in the bathroom so often!

One particular day, Denise mentioned she was feeling particularly uneasy so she went off to her usual prayer spot, the bathroom. As she began to interact with the Lord, she said she received this strength and peace, which she could not explain. She then returned to her desk. She said she didn't know any more about the business yet she was very peaceful. Then, one hour later, chaos broke out.

She received a call from an important prospect that the company had been working with in trying to secure their business. Nobody else was available to answer the call and this prospect was demanding some answers, otherwise he was going to take his business elsewhere. As a result, Denise needed to make some quick decisions on the spot. When this man began to rattle off questions to her, she said she knew exactly what to say, even though she didn't know the business. A few minutes after hanging up, one of the owners found out about her call and was stunned to find out that she had been asked these questions. He thought for sure that Denise had blown it. When she revealed what she had shared, he said, "How did you know that? There is no way you could have that knowledge. Only a couple of us here know that." She told him how God was guiding her. The company ended up getting his business.

I share this with you for several reasons. First, intimacy with God is a 24/7 proposition, something we can have any place at any time...even in a bathroom! Second, fostering intimacy will look different for each of us. Remember, if we seek God with all our heart, He promises that we will find Him. Third, spending time in His presence can be the best preparation for whatever lies ahead. Finally, when we are diligent in seeking Him, He will provide us with peace.

I want to reiterate that, for me, seeking intimacy has been an ongoing process. However, the first step in that process for me was a decision, a decision to seek Him with everything I have.

## Hiding in the Garden

In Genesis, prior to their disobedience, Adam and Eve experienced a true, intimate relationship with God. They shared everything with Him. It had to be amazing. But after they ate of the forbidden tree, look at what happened:

> When the woman saw that the fruit of the tree was good for food and pleasing to the eye, and also desirable for gaining wisdom, she took some and ate it. She also gave some to her husband, who was with her, and he ate it. Then the eyes of both of them were opened, and they realized they were naked; so they sewed fig leaves together and made coverings for themselves.

> Then the man and his wife heard the sound of the LORD
> God as he was walking in the garden in the cool of the day,
> and they hid from the LORD God among the trees of the
> garden. But the LORD God called to the man, "Where are
> you?"
> He answered, "I heard you in the garden, and I was afraid
> because I was naked; so I hid." (Genesis 3:6-10)

Upon sinning, the first thing they did was cover themselves. We do the same thing when we put up our defenses, our walls, our masks. We don't want others to see the "real" us for fear that they might no longer accept or respect us any if they really knew us. The strange thing about this is that when someone openly shares with me from a place of vulnerability, I always have a deeper level of respect for him or her. So believing that keeping things to yourself will help others maintain their respect for you is a lie. In addition, when we become vulnerable we find true healing. I have experienced this personally and I see it repeatedly in the leadership roundtable groups I lead. When people share their true selves, they feel an enormous weight lifted from their shoulders and the healing begins.

The second thing Adam and Eve did was to hide from God. When I was in the second grade, I tried to chop down a rather large tree in our front yard with an axe. I was unsuccessful but I did some serious damage to the tree. To top it off, that same day I also threw rocks at our neighbor's brand new car. My mom caught me and said that I would need to explain my escapades to my father. I was in agony that day awaiting my dad's arrival from work, so I hid. Whether or not you have experienced something similar in your life, most of us have, to some extent, done this with God. We often hide from Him, thinking that we are in big trouble and don't want to face the consequences or that He won't accept us because of our wrongs. No matter the reason, as my dad found me that terrible evening so many years ago, God will find you. He knows everything, even the stuff you try to keep hidden.

He wants us to come to Him in everything. He wants us to know Him and He wants to know us at the core of our being. He wants us fully surrendered to Him. That is intimacy. I have found Psalm 139:23-24 to be a great prayer in helping God know my heart and I think you will too: *Search me, O God, and know my heart; test me and know my anxious thoughts. See if there is any offensive way in me, and lead me in the way everlasting.*

## Enjoying God

A few days ago, I went on one of my monthly retreat days and had an incredible time with God. It might sound a bit strange, but it may have been one of the most enjoyable days of my life. Let me explain. As I have entered into this journey to seek God with all my heart, I have been learning something foundational. I have found myself not being concerned so much with the *how* as much as the *Who.* I may enter a retreat with a plan of sorts of what the day might look like or what I hope to hear from God about, but lately my retreat days haven't come close to resembling my plan.

During this particular retreat, I found myself just enjoying God. I can't really explain it but I found enjoyment in everything. I enjoyed watching a squirrel walk along the rail of a fence outside my window. I enjoyed watching him occasionally rub his face on the rough wood. Then I enjoyed watching this same squirrel play a modified game of tag with a friend of his—I was very entertained and quite content. I felt as if God allowed them to be there simply for my enjoyment. Then, for the first time in my life, I literally enjoyed peeling an orange. I thought about the details that make up an orange and the Creator behind those details: the distinct tangy taste, the ease of peeling, the white pulp just inside the peel and the fact that it is conveniently sectioned to make it easy to eat. This particular orange may have tasted better than any I had eaten previously! I felt as if God had made *that* orange just so I could enjoy it that day! Then as I went for a walk, I noticed details in the trees and animals that left me awestruck at God's power and love for me.

This went on for the entire day. Did I receive any startling revelation that day? No, not that I'm aware of. Did I hear anything about the issues I was wrestling with? Not directly. But, I was reminded that God is my best Friend and I got to spend the day with Him—and it felt wonderful! As mentioned, in the past I might have thought this to be a waste of time because it wasn't very "productive." Now I want more of this time with Him and I'm beginning to view it as the most productive thing I can do.

## The White Paper Test

If intimacy with God promises to be so great, why do we struggle so much with getting there? Apathy is certainly one of the reasons. *Things are fine so why rock the boat?* Another reason is laziness. Many of us just don't want to put forth the effort to know God. *I don't feel like doing that!* An additional thing which can keep us in our comfort zones is the busyness of life. *Who has time to spend it with God?*

Maybe the biggest thing standing in the way of knowing God better, of really having an intimate relationship with Him, likely is something we discussed in earlier chapters...our desire for control.

My friend Dan works with addicts. Before working with them, he gives them each a "white paper test" to see if they are ready to start the healing process. When I asked him what that test looks like, Dan shared that he places a blank white sheet of paper in front of them and asks them to honestly write down everything they are not willing to do.

If anything is on that paper at the end of the test, Dan says that they are not ready to move forward. Whatever is written down is standing between the addict and the beginning of the healing process. In essence, if anything is on their paper they are trying to retain control and, until that control is relinquished, they are not ready to proceed.

Jesus also gave white paper tests:

As Jesus started on his way, a man ran up to him and fell on his knees before him. "Good teacher," he asked, "what must I do to inherit eternal life?"

"Why do you call me good?" Jesus answered. "No one is good—except God alone. You know the commandments: 'Do not murder, do not commit adultery, do not steal, do not give false testimony, do not defraud, honor your father and mother.'"

"Teacher," he declared, "all these I have kept since I was a boy."

Jesus looked at him and loved him. "One thing you lack," he said. "Go, sell everything you have and give to the poor, and you will have treasure in Heaven. Then come, follow me."

At this the man's face fell. He went away sad, because he had great wealth.

Jesus looked around and said to his disciples, "How hard it is for the rich to enter the kingdom of God!" (Mark 10:17-23)

Essentially, the rich young ruler wrote down, "give up my wealth" on his white paper. As a result, that stood between him and Jesus and eternal life. Again, he was unwilling to relinquish control.

Let's look at one more story, the story of someone who had nothing on his "white paper":

So Elijah went from there and found Elisha son of Shaphat. He was plowing with twelve yoke of oxen, and he himself was driving the twelfth pair. Elijah went up to him and threw his cloak around him. Elisha then left his oxen and ran after Elijah. "Let me kiss my father and mother good-bye," he said, "and then I will come with you."

"Go back," Elijah replied. "What have I done to you?"

So Elisha left him and went back. He took his yoke of oxen and slaughtered them. He burned the plowing equipment to cook the meat and gave it to the people, and they ate. Then he set out to follow Elijah and became his attendant. (1 Kings 19:19-21)

Elisha was evidently a farmer. Elijah came to him and anointed Elisha as a prophet to succeed him as the Lord had instructed (see 1 Kings 19:16). Elisha, knowing that he was being "called," burned his plowing equipment and slaughtered his oxen. This was no small matter, as these represented his career. Think about how wrapped up we can get in our own careers...in many cases what we do defines us (which is unhealthy, by the way). Yet, Elisha basically said, "I'm all in—I'm giving up control. I'm burning the bridge to my old life." He was showing that he had nothing on his white paper.

Will you commit to seeking to keep your "white paper" clean? Are you, like Elisha, willing to "burn your plowing equipment and slaughter your oxen"? My hope and prayer is that the following chapters will strengthen your resolve and your faith so that you will choose to do what it takes to make Jesus the King of your life.

## Acceptance

In the previous parable about the rich young ruler, Jesus spoke some tough words to this young man. He didn't like what Jesus had to say so he went away sad. On the surface, it may appear that Jesus was turning this man away but that is not true at all. Jesus was showing him the way to eternal life; the young man simply chose not to follow that path. Jesus did not condemn nor reject him. Jesus was actually showing His full love and acceptance of him (see Mark 10:21). This is important. Jesus fully accepted and loved this young man and He fully accepts and loves you—right where you are.

Let me repeat that. God fully accepts and loves you, right now, regardless of what you have done in the past, regardless of what others have said about you and regardless of how you view yourself. When you ask Him to be your Leader, the old you actually dies and is replaced by a "new creation":

> Therefore, if anyone is in Christ, he is a new creation; the old has gone, the new has come! (2 Corinthians 5:17)

You are not identified by what you do or by what you've done. You are identified by who you are, which begins at birth. My children were all born into my family so they are all Langes. No matter what they do, they will always be a Lange. That's who they are. From the moment they entered this world, I fully accepted and loved them. They couldn't do anything that would make me remove that love and acceptance. In the same way, if you are a Christ-follower, you have been born into the family of God (in other words, you are "born again"). You are a new creation, fully loved and accepted by God.

I have met many people who feel as if they don't measure up or that they need to earn God's love and acceptance. This can be a huge hindrance to experiencing peace. If you struggle with this concept, I encourage you to meditate on 2 Corinthians 5:17 regularly. The fact is that you are a child of the Most High God. You are royalty. You are fully accepted and God loves you so much.

## The Choice is Yours

I just got through cutting my lawn. Normally not very newsworthy, so why am I telling you about it? Well, I previously mowed it only four days ago. Yet I returned this afternoon from a short trip to a lawn that looked more like a jungle. I couldn't believe how much it had grown. I guess constant rain and warm temperatures will do that.

Because it was so thick and long, I needed to stop to empty the bag much more often than normal. In addition, the grass was getting clogged in the chute which was leaving grass clumps all over the lawn. I found myself grumbling about why the darned grass was growing so fast. Then I realized that I was one of the reasons. You see, rain and warm weather aren't the only contributing factors to rapid growth; fertilizer also helps. And, I have faithfully fertilized. Why? Because I like a green, thick lawn...which is exactly what I have right now. Yet, I was complaining. I guess I just didn't want to pay the price for this type of lawn and put in the hard work that is necessary to have it...at least not today.

This is very similar to our walk with God. Most of us want an intimate, loving relationship with our Heavenly Father. We want peace. We want joy. We want guidance and protection. Yet, many of us, especially those of us who are busy, are not willing to pay the price of intimacy...time. That's right, it takes time to get to know God–there is no shortcut.

All God wants is you...all of you. This is THE MOST IMPOR-TANT thing to Him. That's right, His first and greatest command-ment to you (and to me) is to love Him with all your heart, soul, mind and strength–above all else (see Matthew 22:37-38). So you have a choice to make. You can ignore this call to intimacy with God and read the rest of this book and learn some principles that will help you find peace and that will be good. Or you can decide right now that you will make God a priority and set aside regular time to be with Him and to abide in Him.

If you choose the latter and decide that you will pursue an inti-mate relationship with God and you incorporate the principles shared in the pages to come, I can promise you that you will be blessed beyond measure. In fact, as an added bonus, Hebrews 11:6 tells us that we have rewards awaiting us if we earnestly seek God: *And without faith it is impossible to please God, because anyone who comes to him must believe that he exists and that <u>he rewards those who earnestly seek him</u>* (emphasis added). The rewards we are promised are not spelled out, but certainly one of them is peace. Jesus said, "In Me you may have peace" (John 16:33a). So we need to get to know Him to find this peace. The price we must pay is time with Him.

What if you find yourself at a place where you know it would be good to seek God, but your heart's just not in it. Perhaps the thought of it bores you. Maybe it scares you. Or you're thinking you just don't have enough time for that stuff.

If you are in this place, I have some quick encouragement for you. Seek Him anyway. Admit to God how you feel...after all, you won't be surprising Him with something He doesn't already know.

Ask Him to create in you a heart that desires Him. Even if you don't feel like it, step out in faith believing in God's promises and seek Him until He gives you the desire to spend time with Him.

Do this regularly and I think you will find yourself with a renewed love for God and an increased level of peace in your life:

1. Pray, asking God to increase your desire for Him;
2. In faith, begin spending time with Him and your desire for Him will increase.

Remember, God knows your heart and He promises that if you seek Him with all of it, you will find Him, the God of peace (see Jeremiah 29:13-14).

 **Takeaway:**
Intimacy with our Heavenly Father is critical to finding a life filled with peace.

## Prayer

Father God, thank you for Your presence and the way You are making Yourself more and more real in my life. Thank You for Your Son Jesus. I now know that I need Him if I am going to achieve peace, true peace. Jesus, please not only be resident in me, but be my President...the CEO of my life. Change my heart and put in me a desire to want to know You more intimately. I want all of You Lord! Draw me close and help me to trust fully in You... help my "White Paper" to be clean! Amen.

# SEVEN

# Obedience

*"If you love me, you will obey what I command."*
John 14:15

*"My future is righteousness."*
Bob Marley

*F*or every action there is an equal and opposite reaction. This is something most of us learn in physics class. It is Newton's Law of Reciprocal Actions.

*You can dance all night but you'll have to pay the fiddler in the morning.* You may or may not be familiar with *this* law. It is My Dad's Law of Staying out Late (and doing no good). Back in my younger days when I was leading a fairly "carefree" lifestyle (to put it mildly), my dad would share these words of wisdom. I was not a fan of these words, probably because they were typically being received in the midst of a splitting headache. However, the real reason I didn't like his words was that I knew they were the truth and I didn't want to know *that* truth.

Both Newton's Law and My Dad's Law share something poignant about life: there are consequences to our choices and our actions. The tough part about this is that our Heavenly Father chose to give us free will, to choose whatever we would like, good or bad. Sometimes we will choose the correct path and at other times, we will not. The cool thing is that God's love for us won't change because of our choices—He loves us regardless of what we choose to do and is willing to forgive us no matter what we have done, even if it is something terrible.

Though He forgives us, we will still face the consequences of our actions, we will need to "pay the fiddler in the morning." The book of Proverbs is chock-full of wisdom and advice about the choices we should make and the consequences we will face if we go down the wrong path. Here are a few examples:

- For the lips of an adulteress drip honey, and her speech is smoother than oil; but in the end she is bitter as gall, sharp as a double-edged sword. Her feet go down to death; her steps lead straight to the grave. (5:3-6)
- So is he who sleeps with another man's wife; no one who touches her will go unpunished. (6:29)
- But whoever fails to find me (wisdom) harms himself; all who hate me love death. (8:36)
- Whoever corrects a mocker invites insult; whoever rebukes a wicked man incurs abuse. (9:7)
- Lazy hands make a man poor. (10:4a)
- When pride comes, then comes disgrace. (11:2a)
- Haste leads to poverty. (21:5b)

What I like so much about the book of Proverbs is that, while it contains many warnings, there are even more words of wisdom about the blessings we will see when we choose the righteous path or the path of obeying God. The bottom line is that our choices matter in determining our future circumstances.

King David found this out the hard way. Here is a brief summary of one of his poor choices (from 2 Samuel 11-12):

King David is out for a stroll on the palace roof and spots a babe named Bathsheba bathing on her roof and he says to his men, "Go get her for me."

She comes and sleeps with David. David later finds out she's pregnant so he hatches this scheme to cover it up by bringing her husband, Uriah, home from the battle so Uriah could sleep with his wife. This way when she delivered, everyone would think that Uriah was the father and disaster would be averted.

However, David didn't count on Uriah being such a man of integrity. Uriah said that he would not go to his wife because that would be unfair to his men who are sleeping in open fields while he is with his wife.

So David has to go to Plan B and sends instructions with Uriah back to the front lines. These instructions are Uriah's death warrant, telling the commander to have Uriah killed.

After Uriah's death, David takes Bathsheba as his wife. He has cleverly avoided letting anyone find out about his deed, or so he thinks.

However, God knows all about it and He is not pleased. He sends a prophet named Nathan to share a story with David and David sees that he has sinned:

> Then David said to Nathan, "I have sinned against the LORD."
> Nathan replied, "The LORD has taken away your sin. You are not going to die. But because by doing this you have made the enemies of the LORD show utter contempt, the son born to you will die." (2 Samuel 12:13-14)

God removed the sin from David but there was a serious consequence that David had to live with, that being the death of his son. It's no different with us. Our choices have a great impact upon our circumstances. If we make poor choices, we will have to pay the fiddler which could have an impact on the level of peace in our lives. Consider these words, all from Psalm 119:

- I hold fast to your statutes, O LORD; do not let me be put to shame. (v. 31)
- I run in the path of your commands, for you have set my heart free. (v. 32)
- Direct me in the path of your commands, for there I find delight. (v. 35)
- I will walk about in freedom, for I have sought out your precepts. (v. 45)
- Before I was afflicted I went astray, but now I obey your word. (v. 67)
- May my heart be blameless toward your decrees, that I may not be put to shame. (v. 80)
- If your law had not been my delight, I would have perished in my affliction. (v. 92)
- I will never forget your precepts, for by them you have preserved my life. (v. 93)

Each of these says pretty much the same thing. If we follow Jesus and what He's telling us, we will be better off. Though God does use negative circumstances in our lives to teach us and draw us toward Him, He would much rather we not experience those tough challenges all the time. If we would simply obey Him, life would be much smoother for us.

The word righteousness is defined by Merriam-Webster as *acting in accord with divine or moral law : free from guilt or sin.*[1] In other words, righteousness is obeying God. We already determined that obeying God, or righteous living, can positively impact our circumstances. But is that all God's Word says righteous living is for? Well, no...

> The fruit of righteousness will be peace; the effect of righteousness will be quietness and confidence forever. (Isaiah 32:17)

Isaiah is telling us that righteousness actually produces peace in us and some other cool bonuses...quietness and confidence forever. Intuitively, this makes sense to me. Those I know who seem to "do good" are generally those who have a peaceful disposition about them. I always thought that was how they were wired. Now I'm thinking they are peaceful because of their righteous living. The previously mentioned verse from Isaiah certainly says that.

As I write this, my wife and some of her friends went to rescue a friend in crisis. She had been using prescription drugs and her husband had lately been abusing alcohol. My wife's friend was reaching out for help so they took her to a local rehab center. While they were packing up her belongings, this woman's husband said something revealing: "You know, now that I look back over the past few years, our life was a lot better off when we were following and obeying God than it is now."

Well said. It backs up something else that Isaiah shared with us:

> You will keep in perfect peace him whose mind is steadfast, because he trusts in you. (Isaiah 26:3)

You might be saying, *Jim, that sounds pretty arrogant, calling someone else unrighteous. None of us lives righteously all the time.* You are 100 percent correct. I have as many, if not more issues than everyone I know. Romans 3:10 tells us *there is no one righteous, not even one.* In addition, Romans 3:23 reminds us that *all have sinned and fall short of the glory of God.* All of us. No one who has walked this earth has lived 100 percent righteously, except Jesus. All I am trying to point out is that going down the path of unrighteousness will take you further away from God...and peace, every time.

You may be thinking, *If we all fall short of living righteously, it sounds impossible to find this peace that righteousness produces. How can we do this?* That great question has an even greater answer. This peace is available to us because Jesus has provided the gift of righteousness for all who invite Him to be the Leader of their lives:

> For if, by the trespass of the one man, death reigned through that one man, how much more will those who receive God's abundant provision of grace and of the gift of righteousness reign in life through the one man, Jesus Christ. (Romans 5:17)

In addition, Jesus' punishment on our behalf actually brings us peace:

> But he was pierced for our transgressions, he was crushed for our iniquities; *the punishment that brought us peace* was upon him, and by his wounds we are healed. (Isaiah 53:5, emphasis added)

So, all followers of Christ are righteous because of the blood Jesus shed on our behalf and all followers have access to peace as a result. Even if you mess up, which you are sure to do, the blood of Jesus has made you righteous and has given you access to true peace. Steve McVey said this in his book *Grace Walk*, "Living righteously is the outcome of Christ expressing His divine virtues through us."[2] It is not something we can do on our own, but only with Jesus' help.

With all that being said, God's Word is clear that we are still to seek after righteousness. So what does this mean? Let's look again at David from our example in the story of Bathsheba. In that story, was it a righteous act to sleep with Bathsheba? Was it a righteous act to have Uriah killed? Absolutely not, I don't think anyone would disagree with this. Yet, in Acts, 13:22b, God says of David, "I have found David son of Jesse a man after my own heart; he will do everything I want him to do." *A man after God's own heart.* Yet, he was an adulterer. He was a murderer. He was a deceiver. He was also a man after God's own heart, dare I say, a righteous man.

David was considered righteous because he had a heart that desired to be righteous, that leaned toward God. When he realized he had messed up, he quickly owned up to it, repented, and asked for forgiveness. He took responsibility, accepted the consequences and stepped into the forgiving and loving arms of his Heavenly Father because a right relationship with Him was of extreme importance to David. It could be said that he hungered after righteousness as Jesus says in His Sermon on the Mount:

> "Blessed are those who hunger and thirst for righteousness, for they will be filled."
> (Matthew 5:6)

King Solomon further added this:

> The LORD detests the way of the wicked but he loves those who pursue righteousness.
> (Proverbs 15:9)

What was true for King David is also true for you and me. We will screw up, guaranteed. This does not give us free reign to do whatever we please, but when we do find out about some sin in our own lives, if we follow the model David gave us which is to confess, repent and hunger after, or pursue, righteousness, we, too, can be deemed righteous and will be blessed.

## Willfully Sinning = A Lack of Peace

I have a huge weakness. I love to eat. I am usually in trouble at a buffet or a party in which food is set out and I can eat as much as I desire. Going to my mom's is the worst. She makes this incredible treat called peanut butter cake. It has a cookie-like base with solid chocolate in the middle and it's frosted with this delicious and sweet peanut butter topping. It has been a favorite of mine since childhood. It seems that whenever we go to my mom's, she has peanut butter cake sitting out on a plate...not good. (Please go to calmingthestormwithin.com/moms-peanut-butter-cake for my mom's recipe.) I usually eat too much, to the point of feeling sick to my stomach. It's all the peanut butter cake's fault...It has nothing to do with my level of self-control...really!

Even something like this, overeating, causes me to have less peace. I guess that makes sense because gluttony is a sin, though it's not discussed much in Christian circles. (In fact, I believe we promote it as if it's not a sin given all the food that is out at Christian gatherings, but that's another subject.)

Exercising self-control is vital in the level of peace we experience. The Bible tells us that if we are not self-controlled or clear-minded, we cannot even pray: *Therefore be clear minded and self-controlled so that you can pray* (1 Peter 4:7b). Not praying is living a life separated from God and it is impossible to have true peace while distant from Him. Self-control helps us avoid sin and keep closer fellowship with God.

When we repeatedly don't exercise self-control and we allow ourselves to willfully sin, we are no longer seeking righteousness. This is a foundational truth: if we are willfully sinning, it is impossible to find true peace in our heart. So we must be obedient and seek righteousness. (Let me be clear: we are made righteous only through the blood of Jesus. But we are still instructed to seek righteousness or righteous living.)

Willfully sinning also brings with it fear:

> The sinners in Zion are *terrified; trembling* grips the godless: "Who of us can dwell with the consuming fire? Who of us can dwell with everlasting burning?" (Isaiah 33:14, emphasis added)

I have a confession to make. I will occasionally drive my car a bit over the speed limit. It's interesting that when I am going over the limit, I find myself scanning the road like a hawk, looking for a police car. If I see one, I will do my best to immediately slow down so I don't get busted. Not a very peaceful ride.

When I'm not in a hurry and driving at the speed limit and I see a police car, I don't even let it phase me. I have a level of peace whether the officer is there or not. I know what you're thinking...*Why don't you just drive the speed limit all the time?* Great question...but that might require another book to figure that one out.

If we turn away from God and His instructions for us, we will be terrified. When I am driving over the speed limit, my anxiety level is higher because of my fear of being caught. It doesn't have to be this way in our lives.

In addition to fear, disobedience to God brings something else which certainly will detract from peace in our lives, namely the work of Satan:

> As for you, you were dead in your transgressions and sins, in which you used to live when you followed the ways of this world and of *the ruler of the kingdom of the air [Satan], the spirit who is now at work in those who are disobedient.* (Ephesians 2:1-2, emphasis added)

In the last half of Matthew, Chapter 6, Jesus addresses the issue of worry. He mentions some things that we often are caught worrying about, clothing, food, etc... He instructs us to not worry about these things, but rather, to "seek first his kingdom and his *righteousness,* and all these things will be given to you as well" (Matthew 6:33 – emphasis added). In other words, if we seek after God's kingdom and righteousness, then we won't have to worry at all because He will provide the things for us we were worrying about.

I don't believe this is a one-time thing, though. "Okay, Lord, I just spent a minute seeking righteousness, now gimme!" This has to be a way of life. We must pursue righteousness all the days of our lives. Proverbs 15:9 says, *The Lord detests the way of the wicked but he loves those* who pursue righteousness (emphasis added). Will there be moments where this is not the case, when we fall off the righteousness bandwagon? Undoubtedly. But like King David, if we can live with a heart of repentance and a heart to please God, we **can** have the peace He desires for us. If we claim to be a Christian and do otherwise, not only will we not have peace, but we will also be a liar as shown here:

> *The man who says, "I know him," but does not do what* *he commands is a liar,* and the truth is not in him. But if anyone obeys his word, God's love is truly made complete in him. This is how we know we are in him: Whoever claims to live in him must walk as Jesus did. (1 John 2:4-6, emphasis added)

If you are unsure as to whether you are living with a heart of righteousness, I have a question for you: Would you be willing to run for president of the United States? Keep in mind the intense media scrutiny of your past. Everything that you have ever done would be made public. Take a second right now and ponder that question. If this makes you squirm, you might have some things you need to deal with before God.

An incredible freedom comes when you realize that you were a messed up person who has made many mistakes (just like everyone else). When you arrive at this place and know that it is only through God's grace that you have been saved, this will help bring peace, even when others find out about your junk. It is because we can't do it alone that we must clothe ourselves with Christ as the following verse instructs:

> Let us behave decently, as in the daytime, not in orgies and drunkenness, not in sexual immorality and debauchery, not in dissension and jealousy. Rather, clothe yourselves with the Lord Jesus Christ, and do not think about how to gratify the desires of the sinful nature. (Romans 13:13-14)

## Owner's Manual

There are two different types of people in the world. Those who read owner's manuals and those who throw them out. I used to be the former who read them cover to cover and then scheduled maintenance appropriately. I must have had a lot of time on my hands in those days.

I don't know what happened, but somewhere along life's path, I made a shift. I honestly can't remember if it was a sudden thing or a gradual slide, but now I hardly give owner's manuals a glance before pitching them. I am finding this to be a costly practice.

Fifteen years ago, we moved into a home, which was built for us. Everything was brand new. New flooring. New light fixtures. New paint. New doors. New windows. The only thing that wasn't new was our old, mismatched furniture.

I was particularly excited about the windows in our home. Throughout high school and college, I had had a job painting houses in the summer. It was great income for a student but very hard work. For some reason, one of my areas of "expertise" was windows. I scraped them, I got them unstuck, I caulked them, I reglazed them, I replaced sash cords, I primed them and I painted them.

The house we were living in prior to our move had windows, which required me to do all of the above tasks. I didn't like it one bit. In fact, you could say I despised it! I had seen enough window issues to last a lifetime and the last place I wanted to deal with them was in my own home! So to have new, high-quality windows was an absolute dream for me. Maintenance free windows, how awesome!

Ten years after being in the house, I noticed a condensation problem on some of our windows, particularly in the winter. A couple years later, I began to notice more moisture on the glass. So, I called the manufacturer.

Their representative came out, and after surveying our windows, told me that the big issue had to do with the seal between the wood and the glass. Had I consulted the owner's manual, I would have seen that I needed to perform routine maintenance each year on the windows. If that had done, this costly problem more than likely would have been avoided.

So, now I find myself with window issues again when I thought those were a thing of my past. All because I ignored the owner's manual.

Our Father in Heaven has given us an owner's manual for life called the Bible. He longs to speak to us through it and He desires that we are obedient to His commands. Yet, so many of us are ignoring it. Many are treating it as if it's a manual for their windows. If this describes you, I implore you, don't ignore it! Some company employee somewhere doesn't author this Owner's Manual, it is actually inspired by God Himself!

Read this prayer from Psalm 19:7-11 concerning God's Word:

> The law of the LORD is perfect,
> reviving the soul.
> The statutes of the LORD are trustworthy,
> making wise the simple.
> The precepts of the LORD are right,
> giving joy to the heart.
> The commands of the LORD are radiant,
> giving light to the eyes.
>  The fear of the LORD is pure,
> enduring forever.
> The ordinances of the LORD are sure
> and altogether righteous.
> They are more precious than gold,
> than much pure gold;
> they are sweeter than honey,
> than honey from the comb.
> By them is your servant warned;
> in keeping them there is great reward.

And look at what is promised to those who love God's laws (His Word):

> *Great peace* have they who love your law, and nothing
> can make them stumble. (Psalm 119:165, emphasis added)

Perhaps the biggest idea mentioned in this book—the idea which is most responsible for you finding the peace which surpasses all understanding—is that it is critical that we each seek out an intimate relationship with our Heavenly Father. This cannot be done without regularly being in His Word, our Owner's Manual.

It is not glamorous. It goes against everything society says. It is not easy and it won't win you the applause of others. However, you cannot get around it. Truly seeking righteousness requires time with your Heavenly Father developing your relationship with Him. Only through this relationship can He begin to bring you peace that you never thought possible.

## Conditional Helper

"If you love me, you will obey what I command. _And_ I will ask the Father, and he will give you another Counselor to be with you forever—the Spirit of truth." John 14:15-17a (emphasis added)

_And_—a simple word, but one with great power. Jesus used it very effectively above to show us a conditional statement of great importance. Because of that precisely placed "And," Jesus is in essence saying that if we obey what He commands, THEN He will ask the Father (God) to send the Holy Spirit to us. We can surmise from this that when we don't obey, we will not have the same access to our Helper. Wow!

"We are witnesses of these things, and so is the Holy Spirit, whom God has given to those who obey him" (Acts 5:32). In this verse, Paul is telling the Sanhedrin the very same thing...that obedience leads to the Holy Spirit being given to us. However, in other areas of Scripture, it appears that we receive the Holy Spirit upon our conversion. So what gives? In the next chapter, we will tackle that question and uncover why obedience is so critical to us unleashing the full power of the Spirit and how this influences the level of peace in our lives.

> **Takeaway:**
> *If we willfully disobey God, He will not give us the peace, which transcends all understanding, and we will have to face the natural consequences, which will further hinder our quest for peace.*
>
> ## Prayer
>
> Dear God, you are so Holy. Please examine my heart, Lord, and teach me Your ways. I want to obey You. I want to live a life of righteousness. I now know that the fruit of righteousness is peace. I know that without You and the amazing gift of Jesus' death for me, I cannot be truly righteous and therefore I cannot find true peace. So I thank you for that! I know that I cannot do this alone. I need You God. Please help me. Thank You for Your Word and Your instructions for life. Change my heart and help me desire to know and love You more. Make me a lover of Your Word. Make this a priority in my life so that I can know beyond a shadow of a doubt what obedience looks like. Amen.

# EIGHT

# The Counselor

*"And I will ask the Father, and he will give you another
Counselor to be with you forever—the Spirit of truth."*
*John 14:15-16a*

*"The best advisers, helpers and friends, always are not those who tell us
how to act in special cases, but who give us, out of themselves, the
ardent spirit and desire to act right, and leave us then, even through
many blunders, to find out what our own form of right action is."*
*Phillips Brooks*

Before I became a Christ-follower, back in the days when I
thought I was a Christian, I would try to read the Bible and it
would seem like I was reading something written in Greek. I would
force myself to try to understand but for some reason I just couldn't
get it. I thought I was a relatively intelligent guy, but I felt awfully
dumb when I tried to read Scripture. I began to think that that was
why pastors were around, so they could read the Bible, study it and
then let all of us less-than-holy folk know what it all means.

After I truly crossed the line of faith and decided I was going to follow Jesus, something happened. I began to understand more and more of what I read in the Bible. It was strange, but true. I didn't fully comprehend this at first but I was very grateful to be able to understand the Bible more clearly. These two passages explain this truth:

> The man without the Spirit does not accept the things that come from the Spirit of God, for they are foolishness to him, and he cannot understand them, because they are spiritually discerned. (2 Corinthians 2:14)

> But their minds were made dull, for to this day the same veil remains when the old covenant is read. It has not been removed, because only in Christ is it taken away. Even to this day when Moses is read, a veil covers their hearts. But whenever anyone turns to the Lord, the veil is taken away. (2 Corinthians 3:14-16)

After a while, I came to understand that this was the power of the Holy Spirit removing the veil that was covering my eyes. I discovered that in the past I couldn't understand this stuff because I was missing His help. (The Holy Spirit is referred to as the Helper and the Counselor among other things.) When someone becomes a believer, they are immediately given the Holy Spirit:

> Peter replied, "Repent and be baptized, every one of you, in the name of Jesus Christ for the forgiveness of your sins. And you will receive the gift of the Holy Spirit. (Acts 2:38 – see also Romans 8:9, 1 Corinthians 12:13, 2 Corinthians 1:22 and Galatians 4:6)

So if we are given the Spirit upon our conversion, why are we told that the Spirit will only be given to those who obey?

"If you love me, you will obey what I command. And I
will ask the Father, and he will give you another Counselor
to be with you forever—the Spirit of truth." (John 14:15-17a
– see also Acts 5:32)

Do we automatically get the Spirit or do we need to do something to receive Him? Yes; both are true.

The relationship that we have with the Holy Spirit is like a glorious partnership. All partnerships are agreements between two parties, in this case between you and the Holy Spirit. Both parties bring
something to the relationship—in many instances it is work or tasks
or roles each will play. The Holy Spirit is available to help you; however, you have a part to play.

I view this relationship like a glass of chocolate milk. When you
squeeze some chocolate syrup into a glass of cold milk, it is clear
that the glass contains the chocolate. But is it filled with chocolate?
No, it still looks like an ordinary glass of milk—with the chocolate
on the bottom. It requires stirring the contents for the glass to be
filled with the chocolate. Many believers today may be Christians
who have the Holy Spirit, but I question how many are truly *Spirit-
filled* Christians. The chasm between what is available to these two
groups of people is vast. As we will discover, those who are Spirit-
filled have a huge advantage over anyone else when it comes to
finding peace (and in other areas).

So in this partnership, we are to *stir our glass* so that we remain
filled with the Spirit. So how do we do that? Here are some things
we can do to "stir our glass" (John 14:21-26):
- Obey God (see John 14:15-16);
- Time in God's Word (see John 14:24);
- Time alone with the Father praying/listening and talking (see
Mathew 14:23);
- Speak to one another with psalms, hymns and spiritual songs
(see Ephesians 5:19);

- Sing and make music in your heart to the Lord (see Ephesians 5:19);
- Always give thanks to God the Father for everything (see Ephesians 5:20);
- Die to yourself/surrender control (see Galatians 2:20);
- Confess your sins (see 1 John 1:9);
- Ask God to continually fill you with His Spirit (see Colossians 1:9).

None of us can obey on our own. In fact, as mentioned earlier, we can't even fully understand God's Word or get to know Him on our own. We can only do this with the help of the Holy Spirit. So it is with the Holy Spirit's help that we can do the things which will lead to the Holy Spirit helping us more. And round and round it goes, building and building...as we continue to stir our glass.

The same is true when discussing peace. There are clearly some things we can do to find an instant level of peace in our lives. However, sustaining that level of peace is impossible on our own. We obviously need help and Jesus is well aware of this. He told his followers that it was for their good (and ours) that He go away because He would send the Counselor to guide them (see John 16:7). To understand the magnitude of this promise, can you imagine walking with Jesus as the disciples did, listening to Him teach each day and witnessing miracle after miracle? It had to be awesome. Yet, Jesus said that it was better that He leave so the Holy Spirit could come. Hard to believe anyone would be better than Jesus, yet Jesus tells us that the Spirit will be of more help to us than Jesus Himself. Amazing.

Clearly if Jesus is telling us that the Counselor is of more value to us than Jesus physically walking beside us, this Counselor must be very special and play a significant role in our lives! It is clear that Jesus links the peace we can have with the presence of the Holy Spirit in our lives:

"All this I have spoken while still with you. But the Counselor, the Holy Spirit, whom the Father will send in my name, will teach you all things and will remind you of everything I have said to you. Peace I leave with you; my peace I give you. I do not give to you as the world gives. Do not let your hearts be troubled and do not be afraid." (John 14:25-27)

Here are some of the ways the Holy Spirit helps us:

· He gives us and teaches us words to say (see Matthew 10:19-20, Luke 12:12);
· He helps us to understand (see Luke 24:25-27, 1 Corinthians 2:14);
· He comforts us (see John 14:16);
· He teaches us all things and reminds us of the teachings of Jesus (see John 14:26);
· He convicts us of sin (see John 16:8, Romans 8:8-9);
· He guides us into truth and helps us to see what is to come (see John 16:13);
· He gives us power (see Acts 1:8);
· He assures us (see Romans 8:16);
· He helps us in our weakness and intercedes for us (see Romans 8:26);
· He helps us to see God's will (see 1 Corinthians 2:12);
· He helps us to praise or exalt Christ (see 1 Corinthians 12:3);
· Help us to live in unity (see see 1 Corinthians 12:13);
· He helps to keep us from sin (see Galatians 5:16);
· He helps us to live like Christ (see Galatians 5:22-23);
· He gives us gifts (see Hebrews 2:4).

It is my belief that most people, including me, do not fully comprehend the incredible power and authority that has been given to us through the Holy Spirit. The Holy Spirit is one of the foundational keys to a life of peace:

The mind controlled by the Spirit is life and peace.
(Romans 8:6b)

## Baptism of The Holy Spirit

Throughout the New Testament, we see that people were "baptized in the Holy Spirit." In Acts 1:5, Jesus told His apostles, "For John baptized with water, but in a few days you will be baptized with the Holy Spirit."

Many times people in the Bible would begin to speak in tongues, or other strange languages, after being baptized in the Spirit. The Bible also mentions that those who received the Holy Spirit will have power to do miraculous works (see John 14:11-12, Romans 12:6-8 and 1 Corinthians 12:4-11). Because of confusion and doctrinal belief systems, there are many who believe that the baptism of the Spirit, speaking in tongues and/or the power to do miraculous works occurred only in the early days of the Church and is a thing of the past. However, there is no place in Scripture that indicates that any of these had an expiration date. Regardless of your stance on this, I want to encourage you to not get caught up in this debate and miss the key point which is this: once someone is a believer, as they submit to the Holy Spirit, He will give them power to do things they otherwise could not do, and that includes experiencing peace.

The Greek word for baptized is *baptizo* which means to be "immersed" or "saturated." So regardless of where you stand on this issue, I hope we can agree that being immersed in the Holy Spirit is something we all need if we are going to experience the peace which transcends all understanding.

## David Got It

One of my favorite Biblical characters is King David. I like him so much for two reasons: one, he was far from perfect—in fact he made some colossal blunders which makes me feel a bit better about my own mistakes; and two, he had a soft heart toward God. He was quick to repent for his mistakes and he was quite humble.

David was a great warrior, as well. He never lost a battle...and he fought in many! David understood all too well the reason he never lost in war. That reason was his helper, the Holy Spirit.

In 1 Samuel 16 we discover that while David was still a boy, Samuel was sent by God to anoint one of Jesse's sons as the next king. Upon hearing this great news, Jesse lined up his seven oldest sons for Samuel to check out. Because of David's young age and perhaps for other reasons, Jesse was sure he was not *king material* so he left him out in the fields.

Samuel informed Jesse that none of these seven were the one God had chosen, so he asked Jesse if he had any other sons. Jesse replied, "There is still the youngest but he is tending sheep" (v. 11b). I can just see him saying this with the wave of his hand, like, "Oh, him...you don't want to see *him!*" But Samuel obediently asked to have David brought to him. Upon his arrival, the LORD spoke to Samuel and told him that David was the one. Obediently, Samuel anointed him with oil:

> So Samuel took the horn of oil and anointed him in the presence of his brothers, *and from that day on the Spirit of the LORD came upon David in power.* (1 Samuel 16:13a, emphasis added)

So from that day on the Spirit of the LORD came upon David in power. David received the Holy Spirit on that day. In the Old Testament, this was quite an unusual experience. Before the death and resurrection of Jesus, the Holy Spirit was not available to everyone like He is today. He was given to certain individuals for certain purposes only. David received Him this day and he would never be the same.

Because of the Holy Spirit's power and presence in his life, David was able to slay Goliath (see 1 Samuel 17) and then go on to many,

many more victories. This would not have been possible without the Holy Spirit's help. The same is true for us. We need His help in order to find peace and obey what God has commanded us to do.

As we discussed in the previous chapter, later on in David's life, after becoming king, David commits a terrible sin when he fathers a child with Bathsheba and then has her husband Uriah killed to try to cover it up. After being confronted by the prophet Nathan, David writes Psalm 51. In the first part of this Psalm David repents and asks God to forgive him and then pleads for God's mercy: "Do not cast me from your presence or take your Holy Spirit from me" (Psalm 51:11). He is showing us what is of utmost importance to him. He does not want to be sent away from God or lose the Holy Spirit! He knows exactly how powerful and helpful the Spirit is.

The same Holy Spirit is also available to you and me...right here and right now. In fact, He is available to us at an even greater magnitude than David experienced. While The Holy Spirit "came upon" David, he did not have the Spirit inside of him as all followers of Jesus do.

## A Life Without The Spirit

One of the very last things Jesus spoke to His disciples before His arrest was this dire prediction:

> "But a time is coming, and has come, when you will be scattered, each to his own home. You will leave me all alone. Yet I am not alone, for my Father is with me. (John 16:32)

Not the kind of thing I'd like to hear predicted about me, that I would leave Jesus all alone. So why did Jesus include this? Was it to beat down these 11 loyal individuals who had given the last three years of their life to Him? Certainly not.

Jesus knew that these 11 men—by this time, Judas had hanged himself—though loyal, had some severe limitations. They would flee like there was no tomorrow. And flee they did.

How could these men, who had seen so many miracles, take off when the going got tough? The reason is a simple one. They did not yet have the Holy Spirit and would not receive Him until after Jesus' resurrection (see John 20:22, Acts 2). Without the Spirit's help, they were not as capable to do the right thing, the tough thing. I have heard others say, "If I saw Jesus heal people and cast out demons, my faith would be really strong. I wouldn't have run when He got arrested." However, even though they walked with Jesus and witnessed miraculous things with their own eyes, until they received the Holy Spirit the disciples were at much more of a disadvantage than you and me.

Even Jesus was limited until He received the Holy Spirit. Though He was God in the flesh, there are no recorded miracles by Jesus and He did not begin His ministry until He received the Holy Spirit (see Matthew 3:16). We have been given a tremendous gift, the gift of the Holy Spirit and we should do everything we can to increase His presence and influence in our lives.

## Paul's Progression

The Apostle Paul. How did this guy who was one of the fiercest opponents of Christians become the guy who would write the majority of the New Testament? It just doesn't seem possible. Yet, a little encounter with Jesus on the road to Damascus changed it all. My perception is that many Christians, if not most, think that Saul (whom God later renamed Paul) was instantly an anointed teacher and that he began his public ministry immediately following his conversion. As one of the religious Pharisees, he certainly knew the law, probably better than any of the disciples, so this seems reasonable. Yet, he had much to learn...or unlearn.

Rather than get out there on the big stage, he first went back to Damascus (see Acts 9:19-20) for a short while where he met with the disciples and did some preaching about his recent experience. He then encountered obstacle after obstacle and found that he was now a wanted man. God eventually took him to Arabia:

> But when God, who set me apart from birth and called
> me by his grace, was pleased to reveal his Son in me so that
> I might preach him among the Gentiles, I did not consult
> any man, nor did I go up to Jerusalem to see those who were
> apostles before I was, but I went immediately into Arabia
> and later returned to Damascus.
>
> Then after three years, I went up to Jerusalem to get
> acquainted with Peter and stayed with him fifteen days.
> (Galatians 1:15-18)

No doubt that this time away was, at least in part, for Paul to process the recent events in his life and to seek God and His direction. After all, his life had just been turned completely upside down! It is also safe to assume that during this time Saul was filled with the Spirit—he was spending this time "stirring his chocolate milk"—which was evident in the power with which he ministered when he emerged three years later.

Though there is no mention of it, I imagine that Saul also ministered to people while in Arabia. It is hard to imagine him being quiet about what Jesus had done for him. But there is no escaping the fact that God had to do a deeper work in him before Paul could fulfill all that God had in store for him.

Paul exhorts us in Ephesians 5:18, "Do not get drunk on wine, which leads to debauchery. Instead, be filled with the Spirit." He is using two contradictory examples regarding control to illustrate his point. When one is drunk on wine, they are letting the wine control them...they certainly don't have control of themselves. Paul is encouraging us to instead be filled with the Spirit and give up our control to Him. Just as there are different levels of drunkenness, we can surmise that there are different levels of being filled—in other words, there is a progression of sorts. This is further confirmed in 2 Timothy 1:6: *This is why I remind you to keep using the gift God gave you when I laid my hands on you. Now let it grow, as a small flame grows into a fire.*

2 Peter 1:5-8 emphasizes the progressive nature of a Christian's development:

> For this very reason, make every effort to add to your faith goodness; and to goodness, knowledge; and to knowledge, self-control; and to self-control, perseverance; and to perseverance, godliness; and to godliness, brotherly kindness; and to brotherly kindness, love. For if you possess these qualities *in increasing measure*, they will keep you from being ineffective and unproductive in your knowledge of our Lord Jesus Christ. (emphasis added)

As a believer relinquishes control of his life to the Lord and allows the Holy Spirit to have control, the fruit of the Spirit (see Galatians 5:22-23) will become increasingly evident. You may have noticed this in your own life or in the lives of others. Being filled with the Spirit is a journey rather than a destination.

Paul's life reveals this to us when we examine some statements by him and then consider when these statements were made in relation to his conversion:

- As for those who seemed to be important—whatever they were makes no difference to me; God does not judge by external appearance—*those men added nothing to my message* (Galatians 2:6; 14 years after his conversion, emphasis added).
- For *I am the least of the apostles* and do not even deserve to be called an apostle, because I persecuted the church of God (1 Corinthians 15:9; 20 years after his conversion, emphasis added).
- Although *I am less than the least of all God's people*, this grace was given me: to preach to the Gentiles the unsearchable riches of Christ (Ephesians 3:8; 25 years after his conversion, emphasis added).
- Here is a trustworthy saying that deserves full acceptance: Christ Jesus came into the world to save *sinners—of whom I*

*am the worst.* But for that very reason I was shown mercy so that in *me, the worst of sinners,* Christ Jesus might display his unlimited patience as an example for those who would believe on him and receive eternal life (1 Timothy 1:15-16; 29 years after his conversion, emphasis added).

Look at this progression again. Paul at first seems almost arrogant when he says, "those men added nothing to my message." Then he describes himself as "least of the apostles" (six years later), "less than the least of all God's people" (five years later), "the worst of sinners" (four years later). As time elapsed, Paul was being more and more controlled (or filled) by the Spirit, which brought out fruit that was much more appealing.

There are times when I feel like I have so far yet to go. In fact, the closer I draw to Christ, it seems like I have further to go than ever. So this example from Paul's life is very encouraging to me and makes me feel like I am doing okay despite feelings which might tell me otherwise.

This also is a great reminder to those of you who feel that you must wait for God to finish His work in you before you can minister to anyone else. Clearly, Paul was not perfect at any point along this timeline, yet he was collaborating with his Heavenly Father to change the world despite his flaws. God doesn't need or want perfect people. He craves imperfect individuals who truly desire to be fully yielded to Him—they will be spirit-filled.

## Fruitfulness

So what does a Spirit-filled life look like? To answer that question, let's examine another question. What does an orange tree look like? Regardless of who is answering, they undoubtedly would include the fact that oranges would be growing from its branches. Jesus uses a similar example to show us whom we can trust:

> "Watch out for false prophets. They come to you in sheep's clothing, but inwardly they are ferocious wolves. By

their fruit you will recognize them. Do people pick grapes
from thornbushes, or figs from thistles? Likewise every good
tree bears good fruit, but a bad tree bears bad fruit. A good
tree cannot bear bad fruit, and a bad tree cannot bear good
fruit. Every tree that does not bear good fruit is cut down
and thrown into the fire. Thus, by their fruit you will
recognize them." (Matthew 7:15-20)

The Bible is very clear on what a Spirit-filled life looks like...it is
one that produces good fruit. Galatians 5:22-23 has this to say regarding the fruit of the Spirit (good fruit):

But the fruit of the Spirit is love, joy, peace, patience,
kindness, goodness, faithfulness, gentleness and self-control.
Against such things there is no law.

Consider what is also said in Ephesians 5:8-9 about good fruit...

For you were once darkness, but now you are light in the
Lord. Live as children of light (for the fruit of the light
consists in all goodness, righteousness and truth).

These verses give us a sampling of what a Spirit-filled life looks
like. However, good fruit is impossible for us to develop on our own.
It can only be matured through the work of the Holy Spirit in our
lives. If you find that the fruit in your life doesn't compare to the
characteristics mentioned above, take heart. While you have been
given these gifts the moment you decided to follow Jesus, these
attributes are not given to you in full-measure. Clearly, this fruit is
something that develops over time as you submit your life and relinquish control to the work of the Holy Spirit.

## The Growth Cycle

Clearly, in order for us to mature and develop our fruit, the Holy
Spirit needs to be actively involved. As mentioned, this is not a one-

Person job. He will not do this for us without our help but rather, He will do this _with_ us.

As discussed earlier, if we do our part and "stir our glass," the Holy Spirit will help us do our part _better_ which produces a flywheel of sorts, something that continues to gain in momentum. As we grow in our relationship with Christ and as we submit to the Holy Spirit's work in our lives, our fruit _will_ develop and mature. In John 14, Jesus also told us that as this happens we will enjoy a deeper relationship with Him and with our Father, which is also key in our quest for peace.

For those of you who are thinking that you are comfortable right where you are and you really don't want to be filled with the Holy Spirit because that might change things, consider this: The apostle Paul, when sharing about how we should live our lives, said that we should "be filled with the Spirit" (see Ephesians 5:18). In order to live the life that God desires for you, being filled with the Holy Spirit is not an option.

## God's Will

I think, in general, we make the concept of _God's will_ way too complicated. If you desire to be in God's will, I'm going to make a bold statement. **I guarantee you will begin to move toward God's will if you do one thing: love God.** That's right, love God.

> One of them, an expert in the law, tested him with this question: "Teacher, which is the greatest commandment in the Law?"
>
> Jesus replied: "'Love the Lord your God with all your heart and with all your soul and with all your mind.' This is the first and greatest commandment." (Matthew 22:35-38)

Read the above passage again. Jesus is saying that, above everything else, _the_ most important thing we can do is love God with all we have. So in God's eyes, loving Him is more important than anything else. It's more important than ministry stuff. It's more important than going to church. It's more important than loving our families. Am I implying these things are bad? Absolutely not. But God wants our hearts devoted to Him first and foremost, above all that other stuff. If we truly love God with all our heart, we will naturally begin to do these other "good" things...but it will be done from a position of love rather than obligation.

So loving God is the first and greatest commandment for you and for me. This means that it is God's will. If you want to be right in the middle of God's will, you must start here. You cannot bypass this. Loving Him is your No. 1 calling.

In Matthew 25, Jesus tells us that if we pursue the call to an intimate, loving relationship with Him, we will have the Holy Spirit. If we don't, we will be in trouble because we will not be prepared:

> "At that time the kingdom of heaven will be like ten virgins who took their lamps and went out to meet the bridegroom. Five of them were foolish and five were wise. The foolish ones took their lamps but did not take any oil with them. The wise, however, took oil in jars along with their lamps. The bridegroom was a long time in coming, and they all became drowsy and fell asleep.
>
> "At midnight the cry rang out: 'Here's the bridegroom! Come out to meet him!'
>
> "Then all the virgins woke up and trimmed their lamps. The foolish ones said to the wise, 'Give us some of your oil; our lamps are going out.'
>
> "'No,' they replied, 'there may not be enough for both us and you. Instead, go to those who sell oil and buy some for yourselves.'
>
> "But while they were on their way to buy the oil, the bridegroom arrived. The virgins who were ready went in with him to the wedding banquet. And the door was shut.
>
> "Later the others also came. 'Sir! Sir!' they said. 'Open the door for us!'

"But he replied, 'I tell you the truth, I don't know you.'
"Therefore keep watch, because you do not know the
day or the hour." (Matthew 25:1-13)

This is a story about preparation. The oil that Jesus speaks of is the presence of the Holy Spirit, working on our hearts as we spend time with Him. The foolish people in this story took their lamps but no oil. In other words, they pursued their dreams (some of which could have been "ministry" or other good things) ahead of pursuing Jesus. The wise on the other hand, pursued Jesus (analogous to the acquiring of oil) as their primary dream. As a result, they had oil, or the Holy Spirit. When the foolish asked the wise for oil and were rejected, this shows us that spiritual preparedness is not transferable—we are each responsible for this ourselves.

Jesus is showing us that our primary dream should be to acquire oil, to pursue an intimate relationship with Him. Those who do this will then have the oil, the Holy Spirit. Jesus paints a grim picture for those who choose not to pursue Him. However, those who do are on the path to receiving the Holy Spirit at greater levels.

## Intimacy... Obedience... Holy Spirit

In John 14:18-26, Jesus tells His disciples that He will not be leaving them as orphans; rather, He will send the Holy Spirit who will help them develop a much deeper relationship with God the Father and God the Son. This will involve learning and loving God's Word and living it out, or obeying His commands. This will lead to being filled by the Holy Spirit.

The Holy Spirit in turn helps us develop a more intimate relationship with God. Romans 8:9a says, *And if anyone does not have the Spirit of Christ, he does not belong to Christ.* The presence of Holy Spirit is necessary for us to belong to Jesus and develop intimacy with Him.

Developing an intimate relationship with God brings us to a place of yielding more and more of our lives to the Holy Spirit. As the

Holy Spirit works in us at ever-increasing levels, we then desire to obey our Father in all areas of our lives. This in turn leads to an increase in the filling of His Spirit, which brings about a desire for more intimacy with God (see Romans 5:5 and 1 John 4:13), and so on.

Here is a chronological look at the teaching of Jesus in John 14-16 regarding this:

- Intimacy: "I am the way and the truth and the life. No one comes to the Father except through me. If you really knew me, you would know my Father as well." (14:6-7a)
- Obedience: "If you love me, you will obey what I command." (14:15)
- Holy Spirit: "And I will ask the Father, and he will give you another Counselor to be with you forever—the Spirit of truth." (14:16-17a)

- Intimacy: "But you know him, for he lives with you and will be in you." (14:17b)
- Obedience: "If anyone loves me, he will obey my teaching." (14:23)
- Holy Spirit: "But the Counselor, the Holy Spirit, whom the Father will send in my name, will teach you all things and will remind you of everything I have said to you." (14:26)

- Intimacy: "Remain in me, and I will remain in you. No branch can bear fruit by itself; it must remain in the vine. Neither can you bear fruit unless you remain in me." (15:4)
- Obedience: "If you obey my commands, you will remain in my love, just as I have obeyed my Father's commands and remain in his love." (15:10)
- Holy Spirit: "When the Counselor comes, whom I will send to you from the Father, the Spirit of truth who goes out from the Father, he will testify about me." (15:26)

Intimacy, Obedience, Holy Spirit. As the illustration on the following page demonstrates, this is a continuous process.

And, the effects of this process can be quite eye opening. In Acts

Chapter 4 , we are told the story of Peter and John who are standing before the Sanhedrin. These were religious officials who were basically like the supreme court of Israel. The Sanhedrin was quite displeased with the disciples for the way they were teaching about Jesus so they threw Peter and John into prison. The next day Peter and John were brought before a panel to be questioned about the healing of a crippled man and were asked, "By what power or what name did you do this?"

Then Peter, *filled with the Holy Spirit*, said to them: "Rulers and elders of the people! If we are being called to account today for an act of kindness shown to a cripple and are asked how he was healed, then know this, you and all the people of Israel: It is by the name of Jesus Christ of Nazareth, whom you crucified but whom God raised from the dead, that this man stands before you healed. He is

"'the stone you builders rejected,
which has become the capstone.'

Salvation is found in no one else, for there is no other name under heaven given to men by which we must be saved."

*When they saw the courage of Peter and John and realized that they were unschooled, ordinary men, they were astonished and they took note that these men had been with Jesus.* (Acts 4:8-13, emphasis added)

Because they had "been with Jesus" (developing an intimate relationship) and because they were obeying Him, they were filled with the Holy Spirit and received great courage.

Just prior to Jesus' arrest and death, He said this:

> "This very night you will all fall away on account of me,
> for it is written:
> "'I will strike the shepherd,
> and the sheep of the flock will be scattered.'
> "But after I have risen, I will go ahead of you into Galilee."
> (Matthew 26:31-32)

Though Jesus knew his followers would flee, He was instructing them to follow Him into Galilee after his resurrection, which they eventually did. After His resurrection, Jesus appears to the disciples:

> Again Jesus said, "Peace be with you! As the Father has sent me, I am sending you." And with that he breathed on them and said, "Receive the Holy Spirit." (John 20:21-22)

We see this pattern repeated in Acts when Jesus tells His disciples to remain in Jerusalem to receive the gift of the Holy Spirit:

> "Do not leave Jerusalem, but wait for the gift my Father promised, which you have heard me speak about. For John baptized with water, but in a few days you will be baptized with the Holy Spirit." (Acts 1:4-5)

Shortly thereafter, they received the Holy Spirit as Jesus had promised:

> When the day of Pentecost came, they were all together in one place. Suddenly a sound like the blowing of a violent wind came from heaven and filled the whole house where they were sitting. They saw what seemed to be tongues of fire that separated and came to rest on each of them. All of them were filled with the Holy Spirit and began to speak in other tongues as the Spirit enabled them. (Acts 2:1-4)

Do you see the progression in each of these instances? First, they spent more than three years "with Jesus" developing an intimate relationship. Next, they obeyed what Jesus had told them. Only then did they receive the Holy Spirit, which gave them great power.

## My Encounter

I want to share a dramatic personal example of this progression. In late 2009, I was in a state (which continues to this day) in which God was wooing me into a closer, more intimate relationship with Him. As I was responding to this call to intimacy, I felt strongly that God wanted me in Kansas City for a meeting to which I had been invited. This meeting was part of the *Onething* conference given by the International House of Prayer. I knew God wanted me there; however, I really did not want to go at all. To top it off, nothing seemed to go well at the beginning of this trip.

Three days prior, I began working out on an elliptical machine. Though I had been exercising regularly, this was new equipment for me. As a result, my calf muscles were incredibly sore and it was actually difficult to walk. So, I was feeling a bit sorry for myself as I trudged through Detroit's airport to catch my flight. Once I boarded the plane, I put my roller bag in the overhead bin and noticed that one of the wheels looked loose. I figured I'd take a look at it when I got to my destination. A few minutes later, one of the flight attendants came by and moved my bag to the other side, bumping the wheel and snapping it off.

She was very apologetic and even gave me some extra frequent flyer miles, but the fact remained: *I will now need to lug this thing around, along with my heavy computer bag.* I realized I wouldn't have the convenience of my fully-functional roller bag. (Normally I would attach my computer bag to the top of my roller bag, which would allow me to wheel it around easily.)

When I arrived at my connecting airport, I dragged my suitcase behind me on one wheel while carrying my heavy briefcase and laptop in the other hand all the while limping along with my painful calves. I think I walked several miles to my next gate. (Okay, that's an exaggeration, but it was really far!) I was pathetic and I was complaining to myself about how difficult my life was.

Then, as I was sitting in the plane on my connecting flight, I began to see my situation in a whole new light. (Actually, I believe the Holy Spirit was convicting me.) I began to be thankful: thankful that I could fly to Kansas City, rather than walk; thankful that I had luggage; thankful that I could still drag it on one wheel and didn't have to carry it; thankful that I was able to feel the pain in my calves; and, especially thankful that God loves me even when I'm acting like a four year-old.

I want to share with you a few brief passages in my journal from the two days that followed:

12/30/09: Sitting in my hotel in Kansas City. Yesterday I attended the meeting I was invited to but I didn't get any new information at all. That meeting can't be why I am supposed to be here! I then went to the *Onething* conference and heard some great teaching by Mike Bickle which will be helpful to me. However, I don't think that's why I'm here. I hurt all over...my back and my calves and my shoulders. My back pain has been going on for the past week. My calf pain is from starting on the elliptical this week...it literally hurts to walk. My shoulders hurt because my roller bag broke and I needed to carry everything. Lord, please help me and show me why I'm here!

During quiet time this morning, I felt as if God said, "I'll show you today."

12/31/09: Boy did He ever! During morning worship time yesterday, through the lyrics, I felt convicted about the fact that I had been focusing totally on me, my pains, my inconvenience and asking "what's in it for me?" I should have simply been focusing on Jesus.

One of the lyrics talked about fame, wealth, power and my name as not being important. Well, I have made some of those things important to me (fame, wealth, my name). I feel so broken.

The next song talked about taking Your place in the center of my heart. "Take Your place and have the preeminence Jesus!" That is my prayer today. Change my heart Lord!

If this is the only reason why God wanted me to come, it was worth it.

2:00: Mike Bickle teaching on loving God. Wow! This may have been the reason He wanted me here! What a lesson for me!

3:00: Mike Bickle teaching on prayer and worship movement. Wow! I believe this is the reason God wanted me here!

7:00: Worship time. Wow!!!! Maybe around 7:50, from the platform, they asked the Holy Spirit to come. Then we all asked. And come He did! There was an outpouring for several hours.

I, along with thousands of others, had an encounter with the Holy Spirit that evening that I had never experienced before. I could actually feel Him and I felt as if I was actually being filled up by His presence—it was truly an incredible thing. This went on for more than four glorious hours. I know now why God wanted me to be in Kansas City.

I share this with you with some trepidation because being filled by the Holy Spirit is not something that happens only at a conference. It also doesn't have to happen while surrounded by other people. It is something that can happen in our normal, day-to-day lives. Going to Kansas City was not the important thing for me. I was simply obeying God. He just wanted (and wants) me...all of me (and all of you!).

I wanted to bring this story to light because it backs up this progression that Jesus taught in John 14-16. Through my seeking an intimate relationship with God, He showed me what He wanted me to do (go to Kansas City). In spite of my feelings, I decided to go anyway and I encountered the Holy Spirit in a way I didn't know was possible, which has given me a hunger to know Him at even deeper levels. Intimacy...Obedience...Holy Spirit.

**Takeaway:**
*It is impossible for us to have peace and live the life God has called us to without the help of the Holy Spirit. The Spirit will not do this on His own, but rather will partner with us to bring about this change in our lives.*

## Prayer

Father God, thank You for the gift of Your Holy Spirit. I now recognize that in order to have true peace, I must be fully submitted to the Spirit's work in my life. I deeply desire that. Please change my heart, Lord, to one that submits to Your will alone. Continually fill me with Your Spirit. Dear God, please reveal to me my part in this and give me a spirit willing to obey. Amen.

# Paul's Plan

Here are Paul's instructions for finding peace:

> Rejoice in the Lord always. I will say it again: Rejoice!
> Let your gentleness be evident to all. The Lord is near. Do
> not be anxious about anything, but in everything, by prayer
> and petition, with thanksgiving, present your requests to
> God. And the peace of God, which transcends all
> understanding, will guard your hearts and your minds in
> Christ Jesus.
> Finally, brothers, whatever is true, whatever is noble,
> whatever is right, whatever is pure, whatever is lovely,
> whatever is admirable—if anything is excellent or
> praiseworthy—think about such things. Whatever you have
> learned or received or heard from me, or seen in me—put it
> into practice. And the God of peace will be with you.
> (Philippians 4:4-9)

As mentioned, the things Paul tells the Philippians to do are not
possible without the help of the Holy Spirit. So why would Paul
give these instructions knowing that they were impossible to achieve
without this help?

The answer is found in the opening section of Philippians:

I thank my God every time I remember you. In all my prayers for all of you, I always pray with joy because of your partnership in the gospel from the first day until now, being confident of this, that he who began a good work in you will carry it on to completion until the day of Christ Jesus. It is right for me to feel this way about all of you, since I have you in my heart and, whether I am in chains or defending and confirming the gospel, all of you share in God's grace with me. God can testify how I long for all of you with the affection of Christ Jesus. And this is my prayer: that your love may abound more and more in knowledge and depth of insight, so that you may be able to discern what is best and may be pure and blameless for the day of Christ, filled with the fruit of righteousness that comes through Jesus Christ—to the glory and praise of God. (Philippians 1:3-11)

Can you feel the admiration that Paul had for these people? He knew that they "got it." They were following Jesus and seeking Him. Paul knew that they were paying the price for intimacy with the Father, were obeying Him, and as a result, were filled with the Holy Spirit. This is why he could instruct the Philippians as he did in chapter 4. He knew that his instructions were doable, because they had the Counselor to help them. The same holds true for us.

Here is what we will explore in the coming chapters...

# NINE

# Joy

*Rejoice in the Lord always. I will say it again: Rejoice!*
*Philippians 4:4*

*"One joy shatters a hundred griefs."*
*Chinese Proverb*

What makes you happy? For me, it's seeing my wife and children smile. Watching my kids play together. Coaching others who want to grow. Watching the Ohio State Buckeyes play football. (Yes, this makes me happy, especially when they win!)

If we all listed everything that brings us happiness, our lists would all look different. Some would be filled with many, many entries. Others might have just a few. Most of us can list at least *something* that makes us happy.

It is easy to be happy when things are going well. But, it seems that life doesn't always allow us to stay happy for very long. Stuff happens. Remember Jesus promised us in John 16 that "in this life you will have trouble." When this trouble comes, it is very easy to lose our happiness. But in the verse at the beginning of this chapter, Paul is instructing us to rejoice, or be joyful ALWAYS. But how can this be?

In order to fully grasp this, we must first understand the difference between joy and happiness. Happiness is an emotion based on circumstances while joy is a quality derived from God Himself. Because of this, it *is* possible to be joyful even when things aren't going well.

Remember, Paul penned the letter to the Philippians from a prison cell. He obviously was rejoicing in spite of his circumstances. In fact, in the previous chapter Paul said, "Finally, my brothers, rejoice in the Lord! It is no trouble for me to write the same things to you again, and it is a safeguard for you" (Philippians 3:1). He not only is rejoicing but is telling the Philippians that it is no trouble for him to do so—what an example!

If you're like me, you might be thinking, *well Paul must be a pretty optimistic guy. I'm just not wired that way...that sort of thinking is okay for some but I'm different.*

If that describes you, Paul has some instructions for you:

- Do not conform any longer to the pattern of this world, but *be transformed by the renewing of your mind.* Then you will be able to test and approve what God's will is— his good, pleasing and perfect will. (Romans 12:2, emphasis added)
- You were taught, with regard to your former way of life, to put off your old self, which is being corrupted by its deceitful desires; *to be made new in the attitude of your minds; and to put on the new self,* created to be like God in true righteousness and holiness. (Ephesians 4:22-24 emphasis added)
- Do not lie to each other, since you have *taken off your old self* with its practices and have *put on the new self,* which is being renewed in knowledge in the image of its Creator. (Colossians 3:9-10, emphasis added)

He is telling us that this is not something we are born with. It is something we must do. We must renew our mind. We must put off the old self. We must put on the new self. It is a choice, not just something that happens. Psalm 118:24 says, *This is the day the LORD has made; let us rejoice and be glad in it.* It is a choice we have each day.

When you step into your closet, do your clothes just jump on you? Of course not. You need to choose what clothes you are going to wear, then you need to put them on. Paul is telling us the same thing. We must put on joy. In other words, we must **choose** to be joyful...always!

A friend of mine sent me an email containing this journal entry written by an anonymous nurse working in a nursing home:

> A 92-year-old, petite, well-poised and proud man, who is fully dressed each morning by eight o'clock, with his hair fashionably combed and shaved perfectly, even though he is legally blind, moved to a nursing home today.
>
> His wife of 70 years recently passed away, making the move necessary. After many hours of waiting patiently in the lobby of the nursing home, he smiled sweetly when told his room was ready.
>
> As he maneuvered his walker to the elevator, I provided a visual description of his tiny room, including the eyelet sheets that had been hung on his window.
>
> "I love it," he stated with the enthusiasm of an eight-year-old having just been presented with a new puppy.
>
> "Mr. Jones, you haven't seen the room yet, just wait."
>
> "That doesn't have anything to do with it," he replied.
>
> "Being joyful is something you decide on ahead of time. Whether I like my room or not doesn't depend on how the furniture is arranged...it's how I arrange my mind. I already decided to love it. It's a decision I make every morning when I wake up. I have a choice. I can spend the day in bed recounting the difficulty I have with the parts of my body

that no longer work, or get out of bed and be thankful for
the ones that do."

He gets it. Being joyful is a choice. Of course, true joy is only
possible because of Jesus' joy. The joy He provides is available for
us even during tough times if we remain (or abide) in Him, if His
words remain in us, if we obey His commands and remain in His
love:

> "I am the vine; you are the branches. If a man remains in
> me and I in him, he will bear much fruit; apart from me you
> can do nothing. If anyone does not remain in me, he is like
> a branch that is thrown away and withers; such branches are
> picked up, thrown into the fire and burned. If you remain in
> me and my words remain in you, ask whatever you wish,
> and it will be given you. This is to my Father's glory, that
> you bear much fruit, showing yourselves to be my disciples.
>
> "As the Father has loved me, so have I loved you. Now
> remain in my love. If you obey my commands, you will
> remain in my love, just as I have obeyed my Father's
> commands and remain in his love. *I have told you this so
> that my joy may be in you and that your joy may be
> complete.*" (John 15:5-11, emphasis added)

## Our Example

One of the things that brings great joy to Christ-followers is to
be doing exactly what God wants them to be doing, to be perform-
ing in their "sweet-spot."

I have seen it repeatedly in my life and in the lives of others and
I'll bet you have, too. Have you ever been talking with someone
when suddenly they come alive when a certain topic comes up? Their
eyebrows rise, showing their excitement and joy oozes out of their
pores. Most of us have witnessed this.

It is my belief that we are wired this way on purpose. We each
have different things that get us excited and that is one of the ways

God directs us toward what He would like us to be doing.

God designs us all with a unique purpose. No one will have the same purpose as the next. It is our mission to find out that purpose and then to pursue it. I have heard it said that the two greatest days in your life are the day you were born and the day you found out why.

God also designed us with another purpose, a common purpose. So we were created for an *individual* purpose and we were created for a *shared* purpose. Jesus' last words to us in the book of Matthew are known as The Great Commission and they describe part of our shared purpose (as mentioned earlier, we also have the shared purpose to love God and seek intimacy with Him). It is what He wants us ALL to do:

> "All authority in Heaven and on earth has been given to me. Therefore go and make disciples of all nations, baptizing them in the name of the Father and of the Son and of the Holy Spirit, and teaching them to obey everything I have commanded you. And surely I am with you always, to the very end of the age." (Matthew 28:18b-20)

This is not a request, but a commandment. We are to go. We are to share His love and make disciples of all nations. We are to baptize them and teach them. By the way, we are not doing this alone; He promises to be with us until the very end.

Ray, a good friend of mine, when speaking to a group will often ask, "How many of you know someone who is a Christian but they act like they've been weaned on a dill pickle?" To emulate them, he will then clench his teeth and with a scowl say, "I just love Jesus!"

While this sounds silly, many of us know people like this. (Hopefully, you're not one of them.) How successful do you think someone like this will be at fulfilling the Great Commission? You're right, probably not very successful.

One of my favorite verses when it comes to sharing my faith is 1 Peter 3:15b:

> Always be prepared to give an answer to everyone who
> asks you to give the reason for the hope that you have. But
> do this with gentleness and respect.

I discovered this verse totally by accident. In chapter 13, I will share a story in which my boss was yelling and screaming obscenities at me. During this time, I was meditating on a verse and I was amazingly calm.

The best part of the story, though, happened that night at dinner. I was with the four guys from my team who were with me at our meeting with my boss. One of them said to me, "Jim, if I could be half that calm when something like that is happening to me, it would be a miracle. How did you do that?" I was then able to share with them what God had been working on in me and a bit about my faith at the same time.

Shortly thereafter, I ran across the verse in 1 Peter 3:15 and it occurred to me that what Peter was saying actually happened to me with the four individuals on my sales team. They asked me for the reason for the hope I had. And, I had an answer for them. Cool stuff.

Understanding this verse helped take the pressure off me. I felt like I didn't need to know everything in order to "make disciples." I realized that if I could do my best to live out my Christianity, people might actually ask me to give a reason for the hope that I have as mentioned in the verse.

In my opinion, the key to this is to show that we have hope. How can we be asked about the hope that we have if we are not exhibiting it? Being joyful is something that will set us apart from most people and will eventually cause others to ask us why we're different or why we have hope. St. Francis of Assisi sums this up well: "Preach the gospel at all times and when necessary use words."

As a reminder, joy does not simply happen. When Jesus was telling his disciples (and us) about the importance of "remaining in Him" and obeying, He said, "I have told you this so that my joy may be in you and that your joy may be complete" (John 15:11). Jesus is telling us that intimacy with Him and obedience will lead to joy in our lives. The choice is ours.

## God's Will

I have heard numerous people say that they want to do God's will. I have also heard many say, "I wish I knew what God's will is for me." Have you ever wondered the same thing?

> *Be joyful always*; pray continually; give thanks in all circumstances, for this is God's will for you in Christ Jesus. (1 Thessalonians 5:16-18, emphasis added)

This is one of my favorite sections in Scripture. The Apostle Paul is describing what God's will, or at least part of His will is for us.

His will for us is to be joyful in all circumstances. We are also to pray continually and give thanks in **all** circumstances which will be discussed more in the coming pages.

That's God's will for us. That is what He desires for us and from us. Isn't it interesting that all three of these things—being joyful, praying and giving thanks—are included in Paul's instruction to us about receiving peace in Philippians 4? I am sure this is no accident. God is a God of peace, and that is what He wants to give us!

**Takeaway:**
We can choose to be joyful in all circumstances and this will help us experience peace.

## Prayer

God, You are the author of all good things. Thank You for joy. I want more joy in my life Lord, so please help me renew my mind so that I may be transformed. Help me rejoice in You always. Help me to choose You over the worries of this life so that Your Word will be able to grow in me and I may be fruitful. Amen.

# TEN

# Gentleness

*Let your gentleness be evident to all. The Lord is near.*
*Philippians 4:5*

*"Only the weak are cruel. Gentleness can only*
*be expected from the strong."*
*Leo F. Buscaglia*

Jerry Bridges, in his book *The Practice of Godliness*, suggests these five strategies for obeying the Biblical command to be gentle:[1]

- Actively seek to make others feel at ease. Be sensitive to other's opinions and ideas, welcoming their thoughts.
- Show respect for the personal dignity of the other person. When you need to change a wrong opinion, do so with persuasion and kindness rather than domination or intimidation.
- Avoid blunt speech and abrupt manner. Be sensitive to how others react to your words, considering how they may feel. When it is necessary to criticize, also include encouragement.

- Don't be threatened by opposition; gently instruct, asking God to dissolve the opposition.
- Do not belittle, degrade or gossip about a brother who has fallen—instead grieve and pray for his repentance.

I have heard it said that it is good to live with convictions yet be easy to get along with. This is gentleness. In other words, it's okay to agree to disagree. It *is* possible to remain friends with those who disagree with you...really.

Unfortunately, from my perspective, Churchgoers as a whole have not been gentle with each other. There are constant disagreements between Christians over whose way is the right way. Some people refuse to associate with those who believe in the practice of speaking in tongues or those who baptize infants or use drums and electric guitars during worship or allow jeans in church. I mean, really? How can these attitudes ever bring inner peace? Can't we agree that we worship the same God, that Jesus is our Savior, that the Bible is the inspired Word of God and agree to disagree on the other stuff?

Jesus prayed this in John 17:20-23:

> "My prayer is not for them alone. I pray also for those who will believe in me through their message, that all of them may be one, Father, just as you are in me and I am in you. May they also be in us so that the world may believe that you have sent me. I have given them the glory that you gave me, that they may be one as we are one: I in them and you in me. May they be brought to complete unity to let the world know that you sent me and have loved them even as you have loved me."

This disunity grieves God and from what I know, this prayer of Jesus is the only prayer of His that has not yet been fulfilled. This disunity stems from people not showing consideration or gentleness toward others.

If you think you just don't have that "considerate" or "gentleness" gene and this is something that seems impossible for you, don't believe it. Just as peace is one of the fruit of the Spirit, so too is gentleness (see Galatians 5:22-23). So, it is already in us if we are a believer in Christ. If you are feeling the opposite of being gentle, ask the Holy Spirit to help you to develop the fruit of gentleness.

## Humility

As I write this, *American Idol* has just completed another wildly successful season on the air in the United States. It has been a family favorite in the Lange household for many years.

As each new season begins, we are treated to an assortment of contestants, some with incredible talent and others who have little to no singing ability. The interesting thing about this is that when they profile someone before they sing, if they sound arrogant and cocky, they are usually a lousy singer. It never ceases to amaze me, even though the Bible is clear about this:

> Pride goes before destruction, a haughty spirit before a fall. (Proverbs 16:18)

Many of these contestants then are shown walking angrily away while cursing the judges. No peace whatsoever. I suspect that in many of these cases the contestants feel that if they are brash and arrogant, this will help them be noticed and get what they want. However, it actually does the exact opposite.

So being prideful is one way to not be gentle. The fall that is sure to come with pride will probably also not be very peaceful.

## Obedience

Our obedience to our Father is obviously of extreme importance to Him. Consider these commands that God gives us:

- And a servant of the Lord must not quarrel but be *gentle* to all. (2 Timothy 2:24a, NKJV, emphasis added)
- As a prisoner for the Lord, then, I urge you to live a life worthy of the calling you have received. Be completely humble and *gentle*; be patient, bearing with one another in love. (Ephesians 4:1-2, emphasis added)
- Now the overseer must be above reproach, the husband of but one wife, temperate, self-controlled, respectable, hospitable, able to teach, not given to drunkenness, not violent but *gentle*, not quarrelsome, not a lover of money. (1 Timothy 3:2-3, emphasis added)

Therefore, if we are not gentle, we simply are disobeying God. And just so you know, in addition to pleasing God, there are some other cool benefits in being gentle. Let's examine a few:

1.   Gentleness turns away wrath.

Proverbs 15:1 tells us that *a gentle answer turns away wrath, but a harsh word stirs up anger.* I'm sure you have seen it many times in your own life. You speak a harsh word to a family member and World War III breaks out. Or the time when you gently responded which extinguished the volatile situation.

2.   Gentleness helps us accomplish difficult things.

Proverbs 25:15 says *through patience a ruler can be persuaded, and a gentle tongue can break a bone.* It's kind of surprising that it is a gentle tongue which can break a bone. Because I know that words can hurt others deeply—*sticks and stones can break my bones but words will never hurt me* is just not true—I concluded that a harsh tongue would be the one to do the bone breaking. However, that's not what this proverb is telling us. This is saying that gentleness can help us accomplish difficult things.

3.   Gentleness attracts others to you.

No one wants to be around someone who is harsh and only cares about himself. Dale Carnegie said, "You can make more friends in two months by becoming interested in other people than you can in two years by trying to get other people interested in you."[2]

## The Example Of The Samaritan

"A man was going down from Jerusalem to Jericho, when he fell into the hands of robbers. They stripped him of his clothes, beat him and went away, leaving him half dead. A priest happened to be going down the same road, and when he saw the man, he passed by on the other side. So too, a Levite, when he came to the place and saw him, passed by on the other side. But a Samaritan, as he traveled, came where the man was; and when he saw him, he took pity on him. He went to him and bandaged his wounds, pouring on oil and wine. Then he put the man on his own donkey, took him to an inn and took care of him. The next day he took out two silver coins and gave them to the innkeeper. 'Look after him,' he said, 'and when I return, I will reimburse you for any extra expense you may have.'

"Which of these three do you think was a neighbor to the man who fell into the hands of robbers?"

The expert in the law replied, "The one who had mercy on him."

Jesus told him, "Go and do likewise." (Luke 10:30-37)

In Jesus' story, three different people walked by the half-dead man. Only one helped him and the other two blatantly ignored him. After three days, which of the three do you suppose was the most peaceful? We can't know for sure, but based upon what Paul tells us in Philippians 4, my bet would be the Samaritan who helped the man. Also, based on personal experience, the people I know who are considerate, selfless and helpful to others generally are much more peaceful than those who are more selfish and inconsiderate.

It is very difficult, if not impossible, to be gentle if you are selfish:

> Do you know where your fights and arguments come
> from? They come from the selfish desires that war within
> you. You want things, but you do not have them. So you are
> ready to kill and are jealous of other people, but you still
> cannot get what you want. So you argue and fight. You do
> not get what you want, because you do not ask God. (James
> 4:1-2, NCV)

James is saying that it is our selfish desires that cause fights and quarrels. Did you get that? It is **our** selfish desires. This puts the blame on us. Remember: if someone spits on you it only makes you wet. It is your choice to get angry.

Think about your peace stealers, or rather the things which you allow to take your peace. In Chapter 2, I mentioned that every peace stealer involves your desire to control the situation. Well, that control is our selfish desire. We want it a certain way and when it doesn't work out that way, we let go of our peace.

As James teaches us, if we become more "others focused" rather than self-focused, it can help us avoid fights and arguments. This obviously is helpful to us in our pursuit of peace. However, there is another byproduct of being gentle which helps bring peace.

Think of a time when you were down in the dumps and you kept focusing on your issues. It's a pretty depressing place to be. What brought you out of that place? I will bet that more times than not, you focused on someone else or helped someone else with his or her issues. Thinking of someone else is a great antidote to feeling down. As mentioned in Chapter 5, when you are depressed and do nothing but think about how down and out you are, this does nothing but bring on deeper depression. However, when you begin to help others in the midst of your pain, something incredible happens. It doesn't seem logical, but the veil gets lifted. You begin to see things in a new light. You have renewed hope.

Consider this story, which John Maxwell shared in his book, *Winning With People*:

> I recently read an article about actress Angelina Jolie. The catalyst for her change in perspective was a script. Jolie, who won an Oscar in 1999 for her role in *Girl, Interrupted*, could have been the poster girl for a life adrift. The child of actors Jon Voight and Marcheline Bertrand, she had grown up in Hollywood and indulged many of its excesses. She was called a "wild child." And she was well known for drug usage, outrageous behavior, and sometimes self-destructive actions. She was convinced she would die young.
>
> "There was a time where I never had a sense of purpose, never felt useful as a person," says Jolie. "I think a lot of people have that feeling—wanting to kill yourself or take drugs to numb yourself out because you can't shut it off or you just feel bad and you don't know what it's from."
>
> Success in movies did little to help her. "I felt so off balance all the time," admits Jolie. "I remember one of the most upsetting times in my life was after I had attained success, financial stability and I was in love, and I thought, 'I have everything that they say you should have to be happy and I'm not happy.'"
>
> But then she read the script for *Beyond Borders*, the story of a woman living a life of privilege who discovers the plight of refugees and orphans around the world. Jolie recalls, "Something in me really wanted to understand what the film was about, these people in the world, all these displaced people and war and famine and refugees." For a year she traveled around the world with UN workers. "I got my greatest life education and changed drastically," she observes. She visited camps in Sierra Leone, Tanzania, Cote d'Ivoire, Cambodia, Pakistan, Namibia, and Thailand. Her entire perspective changed. She realized that the entire world was made up of other people, many of whom were in dire circumstances, many of whom she could help.

When the United Nations High Commissioner for Refugees asked her to become goodwill ambassador in 2001, she was happy to do it. She also began donating money to help refugees and orphans, including $3 million to the UN's refugee program. (She says she makes a "stupid amount of money" to act in movies.) And she adopted a Cambodian orphan, Maddox. Recently *Worth* magazine listed her as one of the twenty-five most influential philanthropists in the world. She estimates she gives almost a third of her income to charity.

Jolie puts it all into perspective: "You could die tomorrow and you've done a few movies, won some awards—that doesn't mean anything. But if you've built schools or raised a child or done something to make things better for other people, then it just feels better. Life is better." Why does she feel that way? Because she finally gets the big picture. She stopped focusing on herself and began putting other people ahead of herself.[3]

Angelina Jolie appeared to have it all. Yet, she admitted she felt terrible inside. Her life was empty. Until she discovered the incredible gift of looking beyond herself. And, it appears that she has discovered much more inner peace in the process.

## A Great Reason

We all have heard someone say, "Life is short, so _____." The blank is usually filled with some sort of selfish desire, like "play golf every day" or "buy this outfit" or "eat that chocolate cake."

However, looking at this from a Biblical standpoint, one could say, "Life is short, so I must think of the needs of others ahead of my own." Or, "Because life is short, I want to be considerate or gentle to everyone." That is exactly what our featured verse in this chapter is telling us:

> Let your gentleness be evident to all. *The Lord is near.*
> (Philippians 4:5, emphasis added)

If we remember that the Lord's triumph is coming soon (the Lord is near) and that life is short, we will be much slower to judge and less harsh toward others. If we can remember this, this will naturally produce in us a gentler attitude toward others. Some Biblical scholars think this verse means that the Lord is nearby. However you see it, both are good reasons to let your gentleness be evident to all!

**Takeaway:**
*Being gentle and considerate brings great power and allows us to think more of others than ourselves,* *which brings peace.*

## Prayer

Abba Father, thank You for giving us such a great example of gentleness in Jesus. Lord, I want to become meeker and gentler, like Jesus. Help me be less demanding. Help me think of others more often and of myself less often. God, remove my selfish ways! Thank You Lord! Amen.

ELEVEN

# Don't Be Anxious

*Do not be anxious about anything, but in everything, by prayer and petition, with thanksgiving, present your requests to God. (Philippians 4:6, emphasis added)*

*"Don't let tomorrow take up too much of today!"*
*Kristin Lange*
*(a sign hanging in my office, made by my daughter)*

There are some interesting verses in the New Testament, which are worth highlighting:

· So let us put aside the deeds of darkness and *put on* the armor of light. (Romans 13:12a, emphasis added)
· You were taught, with regard to your former way of life, to *put off* your old self, which is being corrupted by its deceitful desires; to be made new in the attitude of your minds; and to *put on* the new self, created to be like God in true righteousness and holiness. (Ephesians 4:22-24, emphasis added)

- *Put on* the full armor of God so that you can take your stand against the devil's schemes. (Ephesians 6:11, emphasis added)
- Do not lie to each other, since you have *taken off* your old self with its practices and have *put on* the new self, which is being renewed in knowledge in the image of its Creator. (Colossians 3:9-10, emphasis added)
- And over all these virtues *put on* love, which binds them all together in perfect unity. (Colossians 3:14, emphasis added)
- Rather, *clothe yourselves* with the Lord Jesus Christ, and do not think about how to gratify the desires of the sinful nature. (Romans 13:14, emphasis added)
- Therefore, as God's chosen people, holy and dearly loved, *clothe yourselves* with compassion, kindness, humility, gentleness and patience. (Colossians 3:12, emphasis added)
- Young men, in the same way be submissive to those who are older. All of you, *clothe yourselves* with humility toward one another, because, "God opposes the proud but gives grace to the humble." (1 Peter 5:5, emphasis added)

Look at all of the above phrases in italics: "Put on," "Put off," "Take off," "Clothe yourselves." Each of these phrases can be applied to us getting dressed or undressed. They are all actions that we take every day (at least I hope you do!). As mentioned earlier, I don't know anyone who walks in their closet and says, "Clothes, jump on me!" No, we need to physically *clothe ourselves* or *put on* our clothes. It requires action on our part. This confirms to me that, while God is All Powerful, He wants to partner with us...He wants us to do something!

In Chapter 5, we discussed that when we turn our lives over to Jesus, we receive the Holy Spirit within us. As a result, we also receive the fruit of the Spirit (see Galatians 5:22-23). In addition to peace, one of the other nine fruit is self-control. In fact, it is the last one listed. In other places in this book, we have touched on the importance of self-control.

I have heard it taught that love is listed as the first fruit and self-control as the last on purpose. They are bookends. All of the different fruit won't mean much unless they are rooted in love. And all our fruit won't be very developed unless we exhibit self-control.

What is self-control exactly? The dictionary says this: restraint exercised over one's own impulses, emotions, or desires.[1] It is also clearly something we receive from God (see Galatians 5:22-23 and 2 Timothy 1:7).

Though self-control, along with the other eight fruit, is a gift from God, it is something that needs to be developed. Much like a weight lifter needs to exercise correctly in order to build up his muscles, Christians must also "exercise" their fruit (in this case self-control) in order to fully develop it. In other words, we must "put this on" or "clothe ourselves."

The following verse addresses this by using some language that indicates a more violent approach. Perhaps this is because we are in a battle in which we need to destroy everything that goes against the knowledge of God. Check this out:

> We demolish arguments and every pretension that sets itself up against the knowledge of God, and *we take captive every thought to make it obedient to Christ.* (2 Corinthians 10:5, emphasis added)

We must choose to fight, to take every thought captive and make it obedient to Christ. This includes anxious thoughts. And this requires self-control.

So what does this mean? From a simplistic point of view, this boils down to a choice. Every time you have a choice to make, you ask a question of yourself, whether you're consciously aware of it or not. That question is, *Am I going to do what I want to do or am I going to do my best to honor God?*

You may be saying, "No one asks that question with every choice they make!" Or maybe you are saying, "I don't do that, but maybe I should." In either case, you really do ask that question, even if not consciously. Remember, you may not be aware of it, but the question is asked none the less, at least from God's perspective. And most of us answer by doing what we want to do.

God desperately wants your heart—all of it. He wants to know that you love Him. So how does He know that you love Him? First, He knows your heart, even better than you do...so He knows where your allegiance lies. Second, Jesus tells us *how* He knows we love Him: "If you love Me, you will obey what I command" (John 14:15).

Jesus is saying that if we truly love Him, we will do as He says; we will follow God's plan for our lives. It's that simple...and yet, it can be very difficult. In Philippians 4:6, we are commanded to not be anxious about anything. These are the words of the Apostle Paul. It's as if he's telling us, "I know you want to be anxious at times; we all do. But trust me, you don't have to go there. Choose not to be anxious. God's got it!" He could also be saying, "If you choose to not be anxious, you are showing your Father how much you love Him!"

If he wanted to be a bit more direct with us, Paul might say, "Listen. When you are anxious, you are basically telling God that you don't trust Him to handle this. So do you trust God or not?"

Ultimately, isn't that the bottom-line when it comes to anxiety? When I'm anxious, I'm showing God by my behavior that I am going to handle this, I don't need Him and I certainly don't believe He can help me. That may be one of the most prideful things I can do and that's not good. (*God opposes the proud but gives grace to the humble.* 1 Peter 5:5.) In this case, I am sinning.

I know many believers who say, "I'm trusting God to change this in me," yet they are making no effort to change anything themselves. Do I believe God can change us? Absolutely. But God's Word shows us that following Jesus is going to cost us and it is not going to be easy:

> Then Jesus said to his disciples, "If anyone would come
> after me, he must deny himself and take up his cross and
> follow me. For whoever wants to save his life will lose it, but
> whoever loses his life for me will find it. (Matthew 16:24-25)

This sounds pretty ominous when we look at losing our life. But Jesus is telling us to deny ourselves of what we want to do, pick up our cross (stuff that God wants us to do that we don't naturally want to do). This is where Jesus wants us. Fully devoted to Him, so much so that we will deny ourselves because we love Him so much. This includes denying ourselves of being anxious.

Are you still not convinced that self-control is a part of this? Let me paint a picture using a couple of scenarios. Let's assume you are a business person. You just received a call from your teen-age daughter who tells you that she has wrecked your brand new car. Worse yet, she did not have permission to be driving it. The only difference in these two scenarios is your location when you hear this news and who you are with.

Here are the two scenarios:

1. You are in the family room with the rest of your family;
2. You are at an important dinner meeting with some clients.

My question to you is this: do you react the same way to this negative news in both cases? My guess is that you will be much more peaceful when you are with your dinner guests. Why is this? Probably because you want to impress them and assure them that you are someone who can handle their business. You want them to have confidence in you.

So why wouldn't you be as peaceful when you're with your family? It's because of self-control. You and I are much more willing to exercise our self-control when there is something in it for us (in this case, the possibility of more business or keeping an account). So self-control is really a critical component of choosing to not be anxious. We <u>can</u> choose to not be anxious.

# Power of Accountability

If you are lacking self-control like I am in certain areas of my life, I would suggest asking God regularly to increase your self-control. You might even ask Him to give you opportunities to exercise it. (Be careful. This could be challenging, as He might allow more temptation to be brought to you.) I would also suggest asking God to bring people into your life who can hold you accountable in these areas.

An interesting article appeared in *Fast Company Magazine* in May 2005. The title of the article was *Change or Die*. In the article, the CEO of the hospital at Johns Hopkins University was consulted. He said that research shows that following coronary heart bypass surgery; only about 10 percent of patients change their eating and exercise habits. This is after being told that death is a definite possibility for them if they don't make these changes. Only 10 percent!

The article then discussed a new approach being used by Dr. Dean Ornish, a professor of medicine at the University of California at San Francisco and founder of the Preventative Medicine Research Institute in Sausalito, California. Ornish took 333 patients with extremely clogged arteries and put them all on a healthy diet and exercise program. Then he put them in teams that met twice per week for support and presumably, accountability. This program lasted for one year. After three years, 77 percent of these patients were still following their healthy regimen. And, they each avoided costly surgery.

The only difference between the 10 percent group and the 77 percent group was the level of support and accountability. So, please don't discount the value of asking others to hold you accountable. It can be a life saving act for you and can help bring peace to your life.

# Just Jump!

Nineteen years ago I remember standing belly-button deep in the swimming pool encouraging Molly, our two-year old, to jump. She was extremely cute with her turquoise "babing soup" (bathing suit) and chubby cheeks. She would bounce up and down on the side of the pool as if she were a spring, saying, "Okay, I'm gonna jump! Okay, no I'm not. Okay, now I'll jump. Okay, no I won't."

I would say, "Come on Molly, just jump. You can trust me, I'll catch you, I promise."

Yet, she would continue to bounce, wondering if she could really trust me.

Finally, she would take the plunge and, much to her delight, find out that I *was* trustworthy...I would catch her. And, she discovered, it was FUN!

I would put her back on the edge and we would go through the same bouncing routine, only this time, much less time would elapse before her next splash. This would repeat itself several times before she simply would jump without even thinking about it. Pretty soon, Molly was jumping even when I wasn't ready! This same pattern also occurred with Molly's older sister Kristin and then repeated itself in later years with Robert. And I'm sure it will continue when I'm, Lord willing, catching our grandchildren.

Our lives are so unpredictable. One of the few constants in life is change. Jobs are lost. Health falters. Loved ones pass away. Relationships get rocky. Stress comes like a tidal wave. Our comfort zones get snatched away. Remember: Jesus promised us trouble. We ALL will face it. We ALL will feel like we are standing on the edge of the pool for the first time. And we ALL have a choice. Will we jump or will we stay put?

If you find yourself in one of these places right now and you are swimming in a sea of anxiety, you need to do as my daughter did so many years ago. You need to just jump in and trust that your Heavenly Father will catch you and will bring you the peace you so desperately desire.

Jesus said, "Do not let your hearts be troubled. Trust in God; trust also in me" (John 14:1). Jesus is telling us, "Just jump in, you can trust Me, I'll catch you."

Had Molly not known me, she may never have jumped in. But

since I had a track record with her, she was pretty certain she could trust me. She knew me because she had spent time with me over her first 24 months of life.

## How Can You Trust Someone You Don't Know?

In the same way, in order for us to truly trust in Jesus, we need to spend time with Him. In John 15, Jesus said, "I am the vine; you are the branches. If a man remains in me and I in him, he will bear much fruit; apart from me you can do nothing." In other words, if we don't hang out with Jesus, we won't be able to do a thing, especially find peace.

Much of my career has been spent in the business world and I currently have the privilege of working with business leaders. This concept of spending time with Jesus is foreign to most leaders. We are out to find the next deal, to cut the next expense item, to lead and cast vision. *Spend time with Jesus? I don't have time for that.* At least that's what a lot of us think.

Because of my desire to get stuff done, I have been accused many times of being a human "doing" rather than a human "being." A friend of mine who shares this affliction with me recently told me, "If I had written the Bible, Psalm 46:10 would have said, "*Do more* and know that I am God." It actually says, "*Be still* and know that I am God" (emphasis added). It certainly seems like we are a hopeless bunch sometimes.

Though I am addicted to being busy, God has definitely been working to slow me down. Through this process, I am finding that there is great power in being silent before God, in worshiping Him and spending time in prayer. I am also finding that I get some of my best ideas during these times, which goes contrary to all of my "business" thinking. In fact, I can truthfully say that when I spend intentional time with the Lord, my level of peace is much greater and it's the time when I get my best ideas (obviously from Him).

I am actually beginning to believe that this "down" time is my most productive time of the day. And it should be. *I can do all things through Christ who strengthens me* (Philippians 4:13, NKJV). In other words, we can do anything with Him and without Him we can't do much. So spending time with Him is the most important thing we can do.

God can do anything....but there is one thing that God cannot do. Before you start yelling, "Blaspheme!" hear me out. God cannot go against His Word. He cannot break a promise. God says to us in Psalm 89:34, "I will not violate my covenant or alter what my lips have uttered." Let me say it again. *God cannot break a promise.* His Word contains some incredible promises to us. Most of these promises require us to act first. In other words, if we do certain things, God **will** do His part. One such promise pertains to peace. His Word promises us that we can have peace and it is clear that He wants this for all of us. We simply need to do as He tells us to do. My prayer is that the remainder of this book will not only reveal the things you can do but also help you experience that peace which surpasses all understanding.

## Take the Plunge and Prime the Pump

Consider a man lost in the desert who was near death for lack of water. He came across a pump with a note and a canteen hung on the handle. The note read: "Below you is all the fresh water you could ever need, and the canteen contains exactly enough water to prime the pump."

For a lot of us, it would be difficult to believe the promise contained in the note. It would be hard for me to empty the entire contents of the canteen into the pump for the promise of unlimited water. Such an act would require tremendous faith. What if it were a lie? I could die of thirst.

This is a great picture of the choice we have when anxiety is facing us. We can choose to drink the water that is visible (in other words, try to deal with it on our own and be anxious) or, we can elect to exercise our faith and pour that water into the well to prime the pump which can produce much, much more water (choose to trust God, which will bring peace).

When you and I look for God's hand in all circumstances, God's faithfulness will become more apparent and our confidence in Him will grow. Just like in everything, this takes practice and repetition and the only way to build this "faith muscle" is to step out in faith. So prime the pump—God is faithful!

## The Sower

In Matthew, chapter 13 (v. 3-9), Jesus shares with us the Parable of the Sower. In explaining what this means to His disciples (and to us), He says:

> "Listen then to what the parable of the sower means: When anyone hears the message about the kingdom and does not understand it, the evil one comes and snatches away what was sown in his heart. This is the seed sown along the path. The one who received the seed that fell on rocky places is the man who hears the word and at once receives it with joy. But since he has no root, he lasts only a short time. When trouble or persecution comes because of the word, he quickly falls away. The one who received the seed that fell among the thorns is the man who hears the word, *but the worries of this life and the deceitfulness of wealth choke it, making it unfruitful.* But the one who received the seed that fell on good soil is the man who hears the word and understands it. He produces a crop, yielding a hundred, sixty or thirty times what was sown." (Matthew 13:18-23 – emphasis added)

In the above passage, Jesus says that worrying can actually choke God's Word, the truth. Jesus also said that the truth will set us free (see John 8:32). So if the truth is choked out and not evident in our lives, we will not be free; we will be in bondage. In other words, worry enslaves us. Furthermore, Jesus says that anxiety in our lives makes the Word unfruitful. If the Word is not fruitful it has little or no affect on us which in turn means we are not able to have as great an impact on others. Not good.

Near the end of His earthly life, Jesus also warned us: "Be careful, or your hearts will be weighed down with dissipation, drunkenness and the anxieties of life, and that day will close on you unexpectedly like a trap" (Luke 21:34).

In practical terms, let's pretend you are on a hike in the Rockies and you're wearing your iPod, listening to your favorite tunes. You come across a hiker going the other way and he is waving his arms frantically and saying something that you can't understand because your music is too loud. You think to yourself, *That person is CRAZY!* About 100 yards later, you turn the corner to find a mama grizzly bear with her two cubs and you quickly realize that the person you just encountered was trying to warn you of the impending danger. But, you were "blinded" to the truth by your headphones. Obviously, this would be very dangerous.

In our lives, worry and anxiety are the same as wearing headphones. We need to take our headphones—our worry—off, because it is very dangerous to leave them on!

## Two Responses

I have seen it time and time again in the business world. As of this writing, the U.S. economy has had a pretty tough go. In my work with business owners, I have seen many face some tough circumstances.

Within this group of troubled owners, I have seen two responses. One group chooses to not be anxious and to trust God. I know this sounds trite, but their actions actually show that they trust Him. Repeatedly, I have seen this group be much more effective. They are able to positively influence many more people, they are able to stay focused and they certainly are better able to lead their companies.

The other group has chosen to wallow in self-pity and worry. I've noticed that those who choose this path tend to stay in this difficult place for a longer period of time, probably because they are so "weighed down" with their anxieties that they cannot lead effectively.

The other big difference I have seen in these two groups is that the owners who are able to cast their cares on Him (see 1 Peter 5:7) are "freed up" to take action. Those bound in anxiety are typically paralyzed and can't do much of anything. Most times when in a difficult spot, I have found that appropriate action produces hope, which is the best antidote to anxiety.

## Much Ado About Nothing

"I have been through some terrible things in my life, some of which actually happened."
Mark Twain

"There is no use worrying about things over which you have no control, and if you have control, you can do something about them instead of worrying."
Stanley C. Allen

"Worry gives a small thing a big shadow."
Swedish Proverb

These quotes sum it up pretty well. If we simply did an assessment of the things that have caused us to lose sleep and that have produced knots in our stomachs and shoulders, we would find that the majority of them just weren't that big of a deal. We would realize that we were worrying and stressing about minor things.

Here is a good question to ask yourself regularly: *Is God all stressed out about this situation?* Is He saying, "Oh My Self, what am I going to do?" If the answer to either of those questions is "No," don't you think He wants us to chill out too?

We must choose to not be anxious.

## An Eternal Perspective

A conversation with each of my kids when they were four or five years old might have sounded something like this:

Me:   "I love you so much!"
Child: "Well I love you more!"

Me:    "No way. I love you to the moon and back."
Child: "I love you to the moon and back 100 times"
Me:    "I love you to the moon and back a million times."
Child: "Well, I love you to the moon and back infinity times!"

It would always end this way. I would always try to find something clever to say, but I would be stuck. How can you beat infinity?

*Infinity* is defined as .... "It goes on forever. There is no end."

Kind of like eternity.

The Bible tells us that when we accept Jesus as our Savior, we will live with Him for eternity. I don't think this will be like the eternity I feel when I am with my lovely wife browsing the sale racks for blouses at the mall. This will not be like the eternity my wife feels as she spends time with me watching a baseball game that never seems to end. This eternity is forever. There is no end.

So how does this affect us now?

If eternity is forever, then how can we grasp what that means? I think it's really cool when you have some way to make something meaningful. Like the example of looking at the U. S. national debt and saying if you laid that many one dollar bills on top of each other you would reach the moon. I also once read that the chances of someone being just like you (having the same DNA) are 1 in 10 to the 2,400,000,000$^{th}$ power. If you were to write this number out, it would take a piece of paper 37,000 miles long. (By the way, this is a good argument to be yourself and not mimic others.)

Now those are pictures that give something perspective. Although I cannot totally grasp these figures, I can get an idea of the enormity of a stack of green bills reaching the moon and a *very* long piece of paper with lots of zeroes written on it.

But how can you do that with eternity?

For a moment let's pretend that eternity is something that is tangible. We all know that eternity does not end, but for the sake of this discussion let's pretend it is one million years. To make our math easier, let's also assume that you will live to be 100 years old. This means that in this example, your life is 1/10,000$^{th}$ of eternity.

Most Biblical scholars say that the earth is about 6,000 years old. Using our fictitious definition of eternity above, this would mean that the earth has only been in existence for 6/1,000$^{th}$ of eternity or 0.6%.

In your life, you will be born, learn to crawl, walk, talk, go to school, date, have a girl or boy break up with you (multiple times if you're like me!), maybe get married, have children, work at numerous jobs, become a grandparent, watch your grandchildren graduate, etc... Although each one of these milestones sounds fun and positive (except the breaking up part!), you know they are not free from negative stuff.

When we are learning to walk, we fall, we scrape our knees and we run into furniture. Through those mini "failures" we learn and we continue on and master the art of walking (although some who know me well would argue I am still working on it). When we have children, they will get hurt, they will hurt us emotionally, they will challenge our authority and they may even run away. However, we learn and we become better and so do they. In our careers, we may have impossible deadlines, a difficult boss or coworkers who drive us crazy. All of this can send the stress and worry meter shooting into the "red" zone.

Jesus told us that life is not going to be easy (see John 16:33). We are all going to have "stuff" to deal with.

However, if you realized that all of this "stuff" was only going to happen 1/10,000$^{th}$ of the time, would you worry about it? Would you let it bother you? Would it stress you out?

Let me ask it in another way: if the only time you possibly had to endure something negative was for nine seconds a day, would you let that nine seconds worry you or stress you out? Even if you are guaranteed 23 hours, 59 minutes and 51 seconds of peaceful bliss? I didn't think so. Nine seconds a day is 1/10,000$^{th}$ of a day. Remember, during those nine seconds each day, you might also experience joy, exhilaration, peace, and other positive experiences.

The examples listed above are ridiculous; however, they are very helpful in making a point. If you are a Christian, you know that you will spend eternity in Heaven after your life here on earth. We know that eternity is far, far greater than one million years – in fact, it will *never* end. Our earthly life is still but a drop in the bucket compared to eternity. Even if eternity *were* only 1 million years, our problems, our issues, the things that get us all tied up in knots and keep us up at night are but the smallest of blips on the radar that will be here for a maximum of only 9 seconds per day!

Knowing that eternity is even greater than this, how can we continue to worry? Besides, isn't worry simply telling God that you don't trust Him? So decide, right now, not to be anxious or to worry!

## Buckeye Fever – We Have Won

I was born in Columbus, Ohio in The Ohio State University Medical Center. I must have been dropped on my head right after delivery, because I am somewhat brain-damaged when it comes to Ohio State football. I love the Buckeyes—it is a true sickness! In fact, many of my friends think I need to get a life.

I say all this because there is something here that is relevant. During the 2002 football season, I was fortunate in that I was able to personally attend nine games, including two road games. One was at Purdue and the other was the National Championship game at the Fiesta Bowl in Tempe, Arizona. Ohio State went undefeated that year and won the national championship in a thrilling double overtime game against the Miami Hurricanes.

Though Ohio State won 14 games and didn't lose any that year, the season was anything but uneventful. Half of their games were won by seven points or less including two that went into overtime. As a fan that is passionate about his team, these games were very tough on me. During their tight games, as they came to a close, I felt as if I were playing in them; I was so nervous.

Something I really enjoy is to record Ohio State's games on TV when I attend them in person. I will then watch the recording when I return home. This was especially fun during the 2002 campaign because I found myself enjoying the replay as much, if not more, than the actual game. Why? Because, I knew the outcome...Ohio State had won. Though it might have been tense during the game, I could sit back and enjoy the moment while watching the replay because the outcome had already been decided.

I got to thinking, *Wouldn't it be great if life were like this?* If we knew we had already won, it would be a lot easier to chill out during the tense or worrisome parts of our life, right? Well, guess what? Life **IS** that way for a Christ-follower! I've read the end of the Book...and **we have won**!

> But thanks be to God! He gives us the victory through
> our Lord Jesus Christ. (1 Corinthians 15:57)

Not only is victory ours, but it is better than what our minds can conceive:

> No eye has seen, no ear has heard, no mind has
> conceived what God has prepared for those who love him.
> (1 Corinthians 2:9)

God even promises us that in *all* things, He works for the good of those who love Him and are called according to His purpose (see Romans 8:28). He doesn't say in the *good* things or in *some* things or even *most* things. He says in ALL things.

We have won! Now let's live like it!

## He Will NEVER Leave You nor Forsake You

> "Be strong and courageous. Do not be afraid or terrified
> because of them, for the LORD your God goes with you; he
> will never leave you nor forsake you." (Deuteronomy 31:6)

At the time of this writing, my friend, Thomas Ramundo, is Superintendent of the Southern Michigan Conference of the Free

Methodist Church. While filling the pulpit at my home church, he shared this touching story:

"Of all the times I know God has not forsaken me, disregarded me, left me in a helpless state or relaxed his concern for me, the most vivid memory happened on December 19, 1975. I, being a young pastor, was in my office preparing a Christmas message. The church phone rang and when I answered, I heard my wife's panicked voice screaming at me to hurry home. I sprinted FROM the office, THROUGH the church, OUT the door, and ACROSS the parking lot to our home next door. As I burst through the doorway I saw Noni holding our infant son, Samuel. Beside her our three year-old daughter, Theresa, stood confused and crying. 'Samuel isn't breathing,' sobbed Noni. I scooped our son into my arms, ran to the car and headed for the hospital, crying and praying at the top of my lungs as I maneuvered my speeding automobile through the streets.

"'Somebody please help me!' I cried as I ran through the emergency room doors. A nurse stared at my blue, without-breath boy, then GLARED at me and asked, 'What did you *do* to this baby?' Ignoring her insensitive stupidity, I placed Samuel in her arms, then waited while they went to work. They called a code and people in white coats came scampering from every direction; then two personal friends, the hospital chaplain and social worker appeared, a sight for my tear-filled eyes. Then Noni arrived, brought by a neighbor. But the defeated shrug of the doctor's shoulders said it all. 'I'm sorry,' he said gently, 'we just don't know why this happens to infants. There wasn't anything we could do.'

"That night, unable to sleep, I rose and reached for my Bible. All night long I read it and prayed. And all night long God was with me. I KNEW He was there. He had promised NEVER to forsake me. And He was there. Then, that gray December morning in the snow-covered cemetery a couple days before Christmas as we put the little white box in the frozen earth, our emotions were wintered-in and withered by a blizzard of grief. But we were not forsaken. Not for a second. *For His promise is that He would NEVER, no not EVER, no NEVER, leave us, abandon us, turn away from us, disregard us in a helpless state, or relax his concern for us.* <u>After all, he's not just a God you can have in your heart, he's a God who has you in His heart.</u>"

Just knowing that brings me peace. Does it for you? To close out his message, Thomas went on to tell us in his poetic and energetic style of preaching that we can't rely on our feelings and emotions. The only thing we can rely on is our God and His word. "Our feelings fib and our emotions lie when they don't comply with the word of God."

**Takeaway:**
*We can choose to eliminate anxiety and live a life of peace.*

## Prayer

Lord God, thank You for being so perfect! Father, I don't want to be anxious anymore. Please help me to simply choose not to be anxious from this point forward. Help me "prime the pump" and increase my faith in You. Help me see the big picture and understand that from an eternal perspective, my problems are so insignificant. Bring others into my life to help me keep my focus on You and to help me in the area of self-control. Help me remember that we truly have already won! Remind me often of Your promise that You will never leave me nor forsake me. Lord, I choose peace instead of anxiety and worry! Amen.

# TWELVE

# Prayer

*Do not be anxious about anything, but in everything,*
*by prayer and petition, with thanksgiving,*
*present your requests to God.*
*(Philippians 4:6 emphasis added)*

*"To be a Christian without prayer is no more possible*
*than to be alive without breathing."*
*Martin Luther King, Jr.*

An overweight businessman had decided it was time to shed some excess pounds. He took his new diet seriously, even changing his driving route to avoid his favorite bakery. One morning, however, he arrived at work carrying a gigantic coffee cake and a dozen donuts. The office staff scolded him, but his smile remained cherubic.

"This is a very special coffee cake," he explained. "I accidentally drove by the bakery this morning, and there in the window was a host of goodies. I felt this was no accident, so I prayed, 'Lord, if you want me to have one of those delicious coffee cakes, let me have a parking place directly in front of the bakery.' And sure enough," he continued, "the eighth time around the block, there it was!"

Isn't that how we sometimes pray...manipulating the circumstances to make it appear that God is leading us when, in fact, our flesh is doing the leading? I admit it—I've done this before, just like the little boy who wanted a bicycle for Christmas in the worst way. One night after dinner, his mother heard him praying in his bedroom at the top of his lungs for a new bicycle. She went in the door and she said, "Honey, you don't have to pray so loud! God's not deaf!"

He said, "Yeah I know, but Grandma is!"

If you are like this little boy and occasionally find yourself praying extra loud or doing something else to manipulate the system to "help" God, perhaps you should pray for God to help your unbelief (see Mark 9:21-24). I know there are many times when I need that.

These are the words of Jesus:

> "And I will do whatever you ask in my name, so that the Son may bring glory to the Father. You may ask me for anything in my name, and I will do it." (John 14:13-14)
>
> "You did not choose me, but I chose you and appointed you to go and bear fruit—fruit that will last. Then the Father will give you whatever you ask in my name." (John 15:16)
>
> "In that day you will no longer ask me anything. I tell you the truth, my Father will give you whatever you ask in my name." (John 16:23)

Though He told us that He will give us whatever we ask for in His name, this is not some magic formula for us to have any wish granted. "*In my name*," also means that our requests need to line up with God's will for us in order for Him to grant them.

In what is perhaps the best-known prayer in the world, the Lord's Prayer, Jesus prayed, "Your kingdom come, *Your will be done* on earth as it is in Heaven" (Matthew 6:10, emphasis added). This isn't just some prayer Jesus wanted us to memorize to recite at weddings and funerals to make us feel holy. This is a model prayer: "This then is how you should pray..." (Matthew 6:9a) were His instructions to us. In other words, "Here is what an effective prayer might look like." (See Appendix D, which can be found at calmingthestormwithin.com/appendix, for an idea that might help you to easily use this "model.")

In this prayer, Jesus asked for God's will to be done and He shows us that we should do the same. We are being shown to submit to God's authority, to say, "God, You know what is best, not me, so please do what You think is right." So prayer is not a way to get our way or to get more stuff. It must line up with God's Word and His will for our lives (*"Your will be done"*).

> "If you, then, though you are evil, know how to give good gifts to your children, how much more will your Father in Heaven give good gifts to those who ask Him!" (Matthew 7:11)

God is a loving Father who cares deeply about you—yes, YOU. If you are a parent, you can understand this a little bit. You naturally want what is best for your children, right? Well, do you give them everything they ask for? Of course not. Some things will not be beneficial to their development so you refuse them. ("Mom, can I play with the steak knives?") You deem it to be not in their best interest, so out of your love for them you do not grant their request.

The same is true for us. God desperately wants us to ask Him for anything and everything (see Philippians 4:6). And when He deems it appropriate for us, when it is in His will, He will give it to us. The funny thing about this is that we sometimes act just like a three-year-old who doesn't get everything he wants. We throw a tantrum. It may not look exactly the same as a three-year-old's, but it's a tantrum nonetheless. We might complain and grumble, we might be mean to our spouse, we might even believe that God doesn't love us anymore. If you find yourself in this place right now, be assured that God does love you and He does want what is best for you.

Wouldn't it be great to get a glimpse of the reason God is not answering our prayers the way we would like them answered? This would be a great awakening for us. Would you believe that this is possible for each of us—right now?

Let's take a peek at how God has done this in your life. Think about something in your past that you desperately wanted but did not get (it will be helpful if it is something in the not so recent past). Do you remember the pain and anguish? Do you recall how you thought God was not with you and that He didn't care?

Looking back over your life and how things have turned out, are you glad now for not receiving what you asked for then? If you did this exercise, I am sure that many of you will be very thankful you did not get what your heart desired at that time. My guess is that you can now see that not receiving what you wanted has helped you to be where you are today. You can see a reason behind God not granting that which you wanted. I know this is true in my life.

If you are in the midst of asking God for something that is not being fulfilled now, take heart—God knows what He is doing. He truly has your best interests at heart and will give you only what He sees as appropriate for the time. If you can truly trust in this fact, that God cares deeply for you in *every* area of your life, that He truly wants you coming to Him in prayer for *everything*...even the silly things, <u>going to Him in prayer will help you experience the peace of God which transcends all understanding</u>.

Even if your request is not granted, you can trust that He knows what is best and that He will handle your anxiety about it. The simple act of going to Him in prayer is like a trade: He will take your anxiety and trade it for peace if you let Him. 1 Peter 5:7 says this: *Cast all your anxiety on him because he cares for you.* What a wonderful offer!

# Why Pray?

A number of years ago I began asking this question: *Why pray? If God is sovereign, if He knows everything, He certainly knows what needs to be done and when. Why does He need me to pray?* It was no coincidence that my pastor taught on this subject the very week I began to explore this. It also was also no fluke that I began to read things in the following days, which opened my eyes up to the reason for prayer. Though an entire book could be written on this subject, I will attempt to summarize my findings as succinctly as I can.

For some reason, God has chosen to work and partner with people on the earth to do His work. So rather than just doing it all Himself (which He very well could do), God has decided to delegate, as any good leader would do:

> Then God said, "Let us make man in our image, in our likeness, *and let them rule over* the fish of the sea and the birds of the air, over the livestock, over all the earth, and over all the creatures that move along the ground." (Genesis 1:26, emphasis added)

He turned over His authority to us to accomplish His will on earth. As a result, He requires us to ask Him to do what only He can do. When He doesn't find that person to pray, He cannot move. These are the words of God:

> "I looked for a man among them who would build up the wall and stand before me in the gap on behalf of the land so I would not have to destroy it, but I found none." (Ezekiel 22:30)

The gap He refers to was a hole in the "wall" that had been caused by the sins of the nation. He was looking for someone to stand in that gap, in other words to pray on behalf of the people...to rebuild that wall. Because He found no one, the next verse says that He will have to pour out His wrath and consume him or her with His fiery anger.

In another example, a great drought was caused by the prayers of the prophet Elijah (see 1 Kings 17:1). In the third year of the dry spell, we see that God gives Elijah the idea that it is time for rain to begin again:

> After a long time, in the third year, the word of the LORD came to Elijah: "Go and present yourself to Ahab, and I will send rain on the land." (1 Kings 18:1)

So Elijah presents himself to Ahab, the wicked King of Israel and through an incredible act of God proved to the people that the LORD is the true and only God. (Read 1 Kings 18; it's a great story.) Then he says this to Ahab, "Go, eat and drink, for there is the sound of a heavy rain" (see 1 Kings 18:41).

Though this was God's idea, He doesn't send the rain...yet. He needed Elijah to pray:

> So Ahab went off to eat and drink, but Elijah climbed to the top of Carmel, bent down to the ground and put his face between his knees. (1 Kings 18:42)

Elijah then had his servant go check for rain. The servant reported back six times that there was no rain, so Elijah continued to pray. The seventh time the servant checked, he said he saw clouds forming...and then heavy rain came.

Elijah shows us perhaps the most effective way to pray...to pray what God wants. Elijah was in the habit of being in a listening posture to hear what was on the heart of God and that is what He prayed! (A note of instruction: though Elijah prayed what God wanted, the results did not come right away so he needed to be persistent.)

Another person who followed this model was Jesus.

We are each called to be Christ-like in all we do and as we mature in Him, we will look more and more like Jesus each day. Jesus was God in the flesh. He came to earth because God needed a human to initiate the reconciliation of the human race. (Remember, He gave authority to humans so He needed it to begin with a human.) While Jesus walked this earth, guess what He did? Like Elijah, He listened to His Father and He prayed. He prayed a lot. Remember, we are called to be Christ-like in all we do. That means, if you are to follow Jesus, you will pray.

## Pray With Thanksgiving

As evening approached, the disciples came to him and said, "This is a remote place, and it's already getting late. Send the crowds away, so they can go to the villages and buy themselves some food."

Jesus replied, "They do not need to go away. You give them something to eat."

"We have here only five loaves of bread and two fish," they answered.

"Bring them here to me," he said. And he directed the people to sit down on the grass. Taking the five loaves and the two fish and looking up to Heaven, *he gave thanks* and broke the loaves. Then he gave them to the disciples, and the disciples gave them to the people. They all ate and were satisfied, and the disciples picked up twelve basketfuls of broken pieces that were left over. The number of those who ate was about five thousand men, besides women and children. (Matthew 14:15-21, emphasis added)

You may have heard this story many times. The miraculous multiplication of food. Incredible! Yet, the part that strikes me in this story is what Jesus does immediately before He performs this miracle: He gives thanks for what He had.

When I try to picture myself in that story to see how I might have reacted, I think I would have panicked. When I knew that thousands needed to be fed and all I had were five loaves of bread and two fish, I probably would say something like, *So what are we supposed to do with this? That's not enough to feed a dozen people let alone thousands!*

I certainly don't think I would have been thankful because I probably would have seen the five loaves and two fish as a *problem* rather than a *blessing*. Jesus saw the big picture—He saw these provisions as a true blessing and He was thankful for them. A great example for us all.

In this passage Jesus modeled what Paul told us in Philippians 4: *in everything, by prayer and petition, with thanksgiving, present your requests to God.*

## Pray Simply

If you look again at the Lord's Prayer in Matthew 6:9-13, you might notice something else: it is relatively short. It is five verses long. Ten lines. Four sentences. Fifty-two words. That's it. Nothing real fancy. No "Christian-eze." Just ordinary words spoken to an extraordinary God.

When I first came to know Jesus, I found myself in situations in which people would be praying aloud. There were times I felt very intimidated. Some would pray these prayers that sounded so awesome and so perfect. And then I would be asked to pray. Early on in my walk with Christ, I honestly felt there was no way God would hear my prayers after the beautiful words that had just been spoken by others. I had this thought after my prayer that God would be saying, "That's it? That was pathetic!" Can you relate?

I was so relieved when I first read what Jesus said about this in Matthew 6:5-8 (emphasis added):

> "And when you pray, do not be like the hypocrites, for they love to pray standing in the synagogues and on the

street corners to be seen by men. I tell you the truth, they have received their reward in full. But when you pray, go into your room, close the door and pray to your Father, who is unseen. Then your Father, who sees what is done in secret, will reward you. And when you pray, *do not keep on babbling like pagans*, for they think they will be heard because of their many words. Do not be like them, for your Father knows what you need before you ask him."

Isn't that great? We don't need to pray these eloquent prayers. We don't need to pray long prayers. God just wants us to have a normal conversation with Him. He wants us to share everything with Him, even the tough stuff, even the stuff that seems trivial. He wants us to keep it simple.

## Pray Persistently

Earlier I mentioned that Jesus told us that He will grant anything that we ask in His name (see John 14:13-14) and that it must also line up with God's will. One other thing to point out about this is that Jesus does not say that what we request, even if it lines up with God's will, will be granted immediately. What is unsaid is that it may take days, weeks, months or even years.

I have heard countless stories of people who have been persistently praying for certain people to find Christ for years and years and years.

Do not be anxious about anything, but in everything, by prayer *and petition*, with thanksgiving, present your requests to God. (Philippians 4:6 emphasis added)

Have you ever signed a petition? You know, one of those documents that have a bunch of signatures requesting something. Think about what that represents. In our government, petitions must contain a certain number of valid signatures for the petition to be granted. Paul is telling us here to bring our prayers **and petitions** to God. So if God hasn't answered yet, keep on praying. In Luke 18:1-8, Jesus tells us that we are to continually ask until God gives us what we are asking for:

> Then Jesus told his disciples a parable to show them that they should always pray and not give up. He said: "In a certain town there was a judge who neither feared God nor cared about men. And there was a widow in that town who kept coming to him with the plea, 'Grant me justice against my adversary.'
>
> "For some time he refused. But finally he said to himself, 'Even though I don't fear God or care about men, yet because this widow keeps bothering me, I will see that she gets justice, so that she won't eventually wear me out with her coming!'"
>
> And the Lord said, "Listen to what the unjust judge says. And will not God bring about justice for his chosen ones, who cry out to him day and night? Will he keep putting them off? I tell you, he will see that they get justice, and quickly. However, when the Son of Man comes, will he find faith on the earth?"

Here is a story that further illustrates this point:

> There was a man who went to the doctor for a check-up. During his appointment, he told his doctor that his wife was hard of hearing. The doctor said "Well find out how bad she is before you bring her in."
>
> He said, "Well what do you mean?"
>
> The doctor said, "Stand on one side of the room and ask her something, and keep getting closer until you hear her answer."
>
> The man went home and as he entered the kitchen, his wife was on the other side of the room cooking dinner. He stopped at the kitchen door and said "Dinner about ready honey?!" He didn't hear anything so he got right in the center of the kitchen and said "Dinner about ready honey?!" and

he still didn't hear anything. So he got right up behind her and said "Dinner about ready honey?!"

She wheeled right around and said "For the third time! Yes!"

If your prayers are not being answered the way you would like, please know that God is not hard of hearing. He knows what you want and what you need and He will give it to you when the time is right provided it lines up with His will. But, if it is His will, He also wants you to keep on asking!

## Pray Expectantly

Jesus replied, "I tell you the truth, if you have faith and do not doubt, not only can you do what was done to the fig tree, but also you can say to this mountain, 'Go, throw yourself into the sea,' and it will be done. If you believe, you will receive whatever you ask for in prayer." (Matthew 21:21-22)

Here's a story, told by her mother, of a little girl who gets this:

Years ago when my two girls were small, they were taught how to pray before eating their meal. One night as I was busy scurrying around the kitchen, I told them both to pray without me. I took a moment to watch them as they both squeezed their eyes tightly shut over folded hands. As my 4-year-old finished, her 3-year-old sister kept on praying. Another minute or two passed before she lifted her head, looked at her plate, and in an indignant voice said, "Hey! My peas are still here!"

So let's pray expecting that God will remove our peas (and give us peace).

## Pray Small

I invite you to reread the verse we're discussing:

Do not be anxious about anything, but in _everything_, by

prayer and petition, with thanksgiving, present your requests to God. (Philippians 4:6 emphasis added)

Look at the word that is highlighted: "everything." I love this because it is an open invitation to bring everything to our Father, even the whereabouts of that one sock that always seems to be missing when the laundry is finished. "Lord, please help me to find my missing sock," is a prayer that I believe would please God and make Him smile.

Think about this as a parent. When your toddler is playing with their play kitchen and she comes to you and asks you with that serious face, "Mommy, can you help me make pisgetti?" you can't help but smile, right? And don't you feel honored that they feel so connected with you that they would ask you to help them with this "imaginary" task? Okay, I know that your first reaction might be, "Can't you see that I'm busy making real pisgetti?" but if you stopped to think about it, it is pretty cool that they come to you. Well, that is how God is with us...He loves to be with us in **everything**, even our imaginary pisgetti.

So let's pray about everything!

## Pray Big

There was a guy who was intimidated by God and didn't want to bother Him with the stuff in his life, so his prayer life was pretty dry. Several of this man's friends were encouraging him to ask God for anything. They explained that God could handle his request (but not necessarily give the man what he desired at that time). The man decided to try this out. So with fear and trepidation he began to have the following conversation with his Creator:

"God, I understand that you give me permission and, in fact, want me to ask you for things—is that true?"

God said, "You are right; ask away."

"Lord, I would like a bridge to Hawaii."

The Lord thought about this and said, "Wow, that's a pretty tall order. I'd have to get foundations set on the ocean floor and get concrete buttresses poured and allow them to dry when surrounded by all that water. That's going to require a lot of manpower and planning. I'd like to ask you to make another wish."

The man thought for a while and said, "Okay, can you help me understand women completely?"

God replied, "So do you want that bridge with two lanes or four?"

As mentioned in the last section, we can ask for things that, on the surface, seem to be way below God...like it would be wasting God's time (finding our car keys, for instance). But He wants to be **that** involved with our lives. While the above comical story about the bridge to Hawaii does not paint a true picture of God, it does illustrate that God also gives us permission to ask for big things, even humongous things (like understanding women!).

As I mentioned earlier, I lead monthly leadership roundtable groups (christianroundtablegroups.com) which help our members grow their businesses in a God-honoring way while at the same time helping them to grow personally and spiritually. These business owners act much like a board of advisors to the members in each respective group. It is an incredible thing.

When a new member joins a group, one of the first things I do in the orientation process is encourage them to write down their BHAGGs. Jim Collins first introduced me to a similar term in his book *Good to Great*, only he called them BHAGs (Big Hairy Audacious Goals)[1]. In our groups, we refer to them as BHAGGs, or Big Hairy Audacious God-sized Goals.

Many of you are probably familiar with traditional goal setting processes. One that is very popular is SMART goal setting (goals that are Specific, Measurable, Achievable, Realistic, and Time-sensitive). We encourage our members to do SMART goal setting, too, but we make it very clear that BHAGGs are NOT SMART goals. For their BHAGGs, we ask people to write down things that are not achievable or even realistic, that they cannot do on their own. Examples might be a family member healed of a disease, their business doubling in size this year, becoming debt free or giving away more money than they have ever earned. You get the idea. Then we encourage the member to pray for this every day.

Each year as a group, we review these BHAGGs and see what God has done. I have to tell you that in the short time I have been doing this (more than four years as of this writing), I have seen numerous BHAGGs actually become reality...from office buildings being built when no finances were available to broken marriages being healed. It has been an incredible thing for me to witness this and it has encouraged me to pray much bigger.

So I want to prod you to do the same thing. Write down your own BHAGGs and pray regularly for them. You will be amazed at what God will do.

In 2 Kings 4:1-7 we encounter a woman who had a major BHAGG:

> The wife of a man from the company of the prophets cried out to Elisha, "Your servant my husband is dead, and you know that he revered the Lord. But now his creditor is coming to take my two boys as his slaves."
>
> Elisha replied to her, "How can I help you? Tell me, what do you have in your house?"
>
> "Your servant has nothing there at all," she said, "except a little oil."
>
> Elisha said, "Go around and ask all your neighbors for empty jars. Don't ask for just a few. Then go inside and shut the door behind you and your sons. Pour oil into all the jars, and as each is filled, put it to one side."
>
> She left him and afterward shut the door behind her and her sons. They brought the jars to her and she kept pouring.

When all the jars were full, she said to her son, "Bring me another one."

But he replied, "There is not a jar left." Then the oil stopped flowing.

She went and told the man of God, and he said, "Go, sell the oil and pay your debts. You and your sons can live on what is left."

There are several messages in this story; however, there is one that speaks mightily to this idea of praying big. We don't know from reading this how many jars were collected. But, had this woman and her sons truly believed in their hearts that oil was going to be miraculously produced until they ran out of jars, they surely would have collected more jars.

The number of jars collected was really an indicator of the size of their faith. And God provided to the limit of their faith (the number of jars collected). This same principle holds true for us. I wonder how much blessing we don't see simply because we don't ask for it. God wants to provide for us just as a parent wants to provide for their child. So pray big!

## Pray Continually

Be joyful always; *pray continually*; give thanks in all circumstances, for this is God's will for you in Christ Jesus. (1 Thessalonians 5:16-18, emphasis added)

Several times, I have pointed out this verse and mentioned God's will for our lives. Praying continually is one of those things that God clearly wants us to do. He wants to be with us in all areas of our lives.

Many might see this verse and cringe thinking that they are being instructed to stop living, check in to a monastery and do nothing but pray. This is not what God wants for us. He wants us to live our lives and live them to the fullest (see John 10:10).

During our full life, it is clear that God wants us connecting with Him and praying continually. I don't get this right all of the time, but when I do remember to connect with God I might just say a quick prayer, something like, "Lord, give me the words to speak" or "Lord, help me" or "Lord, what are you trying to teach me here?"

One good way to remember to do this is to look for triggers that will remind you to connect with God. The more you do this, the more you will begin to talk with Him at times you otherwise wouldn't remember Him. My pastor told me that he does this at every red stop light. When he is waiting, that is a trigger for him to connect with God. So he prays right there. Others I know put sticky notes on their computer or set their watch to beep at the top of every hour to remind them to plug into their Power Source.

So I encourage you to step into this, find some triggers and begin your commitment to pray continually.

## Hindrances

"Is there anything that can keep God from hearing my prayers?"

That is a great question and a very valid one. The way I read Scripture, I would answer by saying "Yes, our prayers can be hindered."

Without getting too in depth, here are several verses that show this to be true:

> If I had cherished sin in my heart, the Lord would not have listened. (Psalm 66:18)
>
> The LORD is far from the wicked but he hears the prayer of the righteous. (Proverbs 15:29)
>
> If anyone turns a deaf ear to the law, even his prayers are detestable. (Proverbs 28:9)
>
> Surely the arm of the LORD is not too short to save, nor his ear too dull to hear. But your iniquities have separated you from your God; your sins have hidden his face from you, so that he will not hear. (Isaiah 59:1-2)
>
> We know that God does not listen to sinners. He listens to

the godly man who does his will. (John 9:31)
    He does not answer when men cry out because of the
arrogance of the wicked. Indeed, God does not listen to their
empty plea; the Almighty pays no attention to it. (Job 35:12-13)

Each of these relate to obedience and seeking righteousness that we discussed in Chapter 7. When we are not obeying God and are sinning, that naturally separates us from God because God cannot be in the presence of sin. As a result, our sin, or unrighteousness, can hinder our prayers. And to those of us who are husbands, being inconsiderate to our wives and not treating them with respect can have the same effect:

> Husbands, in the same way be considerate as you live
> with your wives, and treat them with respect as the weaker
> partner and as heirs with you of the gracious gift of life, so
> that nothing will hinder your prayers. (1 Peter 3:7)

Thankfully, through the blood of Jesus, we have the ability to be forgiven for our sins and come back into right relationship with our Heavenly Father.

> If we confess our sins, he is faithful and just and will
> forgive us our sins and purify us from all unrighteousness. (1
> John 1:9)

## Be Real

I believe prayer is one of the things God has shown us that brings peace, because prayer is really nothing more than bringing what's on our mind to God (and as we have discovered, bringing what is on God's heart to God). Even the stuff that is causing us to let go of our peace.

Have you ever shared a secret with someone...something that's been burdening you? Chances are that you felt great relief in getting this off your chest, as if the weight of the world had been lifted off your shoulders. God desperately wants us to get real with Him and share with Him. He wants to carry our burdens, no matter how big they are. He wants to lighten our load. He wants to bring us peace. Besides, He already knows all our secrets, so we might as well be real with Him.

I look at prayer as faith in action. Yes, I can pray about something, but will I really believe it? Will my actions show that I believe God has it covered?

The litmus test for me usually revolves around my desire to take control of the issue. I want to wrestle with it until I get an answer. I feel like if I'm not in there "fighting the fight" I certainly won't be able to figure this thing out. If I'm not worrying about it, nothing's going to happen. What a lie. Worrying and fretting are one of the worst things we do because we are basically saying to God, "I don't believe You can handle this." Can there be anything more offensive to tell the King of Kings?

If my faith in God is strong, I will view this differently. I will say, "God, this is bigger than I can figure out. Can you take care of this for me? I'm going to lay this down at Your feet and trust that You're going to handle it." And, I will believe that He will and I won't rush to pick it back up. This is where peace comes—when I know that my Daddy's going take care of it one way or another.

When we are faced with something that is anxiety producing, we really have two choices: we can choose to fret about it or we can choose to give it to God in prayer. Fretting is really a choice of pride. "I don't need anyone to help with this. I've got it covered." Isn't that what you're saying when you try to "go it alone?" Sure it is. It is telling God that you don't need Him. That is pride with a capital P. I have heard it said that fretting magnifies the problem but prayer magnifies God. Very true.

In Chapter 3, "Peace Stealers", I shared with you a struggle I have with my task list and the fact that I often have more faith in myself as a provider than in my Heavenly Father. To show you that I am trying my best to bring my burdens to God, I want to share something with you, but you have to promise not to laugh. Okay, do you promise?

I actually have created a new task. (I am a hopeless case with my tasks, don't you think?) I try to do this first thing every morning as a reminder for me to pray and turn my day over to God. It looks like this:

Inquire of the Lord:
- Prompt me when You don't want me to do something;
- Your schedule is my schedule;
- Give me a Kingdom mentality rather than a task mentality;
- You are my Provider, not me – The battle is Yours;
- I want to live this day for You.

After seeing this at the top of my task list, my prayer as I first sit down at my desk might sound like this: "Lord, thank You for giving me the gifts and abilities You have given me. Thank You also for the tasks I have to do. Lord, as You know I have a tendency to make these tasks more important than they are. Today, would You please give me discernment and wisdom to do only that which You want me to do. And the stuff that doesn't get done, I am giving it to You, trusting that You know what is best and trusting that You will take care of it."

If I pray this prayer, and truly mean it, it would be impossible for me not to have more peace.

## To Receive, Ask

- You do not have, because you do not ask God. When you ask, you do not receive, because you ask with wrong motives. (James 4:2b-3a)
- Dear friends, if our hearts do not condemn us, we have confidence before God and receive from him anything we ask, because we obey his commands and do what pleases him. (John 3:21-22)
- "And I will do whatever you ask in my name, so that the Son may bring glory to the Father. You may ask me for anything in my name, and I will do it." (John 4:13-14)

Just prior to this book going to print, I had the privilege of being in Tampa, Florida for a speaking engagement. There are a couple of reasons why this was such a privilege:

1. I met a bunch of incredible people who were friendly, gracious and made me feel very much at home;
2. I got to spend the weekend at the house of Mike and Danielle, good friends of mine whom I haven't seen in a while.

From my understanding, at age 50, Mike is one of the oldest living Cystic Fibrosis patients in the U.S. He is currently on the list for a lung transplant, which will be needed to prolong his life. He was telling me about his recent experience where he spent a day going through tests to make sure he was a candidate for a transplant.

Before continuing, I must tell you a little about Mike. Though he has lived with this disease his entire life, I have never heard him complain. In fact, he usually does the opposite, praising God for the ways in which He has blessed him. He truly is an inspiration to many others and me. As I talked with him about this lung transplant, Mike appeared very much at peace. He has mentioned to me on numerous occasions that, though a bit scary, he knows that God has a much greater plan in all of this, which comforts him greatly.

On his day of testing at the hospital, Mike said he suddenly felt some severe anxiety. He mentioned that during his heart catheterization in which he was in a cold operating room, an X-ray machine was lowered to his chest and covered part of his face as the nurse fed a line up his artery to view his heart. As this was happening, he began to feel claustrophobic and started to panic. He also started to have thoughts about how risky a lung transplant will be and how he could die through this ordeal. In his words, "The enemy was whispering a bunch of lies and in that moment I believed him. Then I said, 'Okay Mike...this is a watershed moment for you. What are you going to choose?'" He told me that something cool happened next. He closed his eyes and spoke directly to his Father in Heaven and said, "Lord, I know these words I'm currently hearing are not from You. I know You are in control and I know You are a God of peace. Please bring me peace, the peace which surpasses all understanding."

In that moment, Mike said that he felt this warm calming sensation through his entire body. He literally began to warm up and all of his anxiety lifted. Then he heard some panicked voices in the OR say, "Are you doing okay? Your heart rate just decreased and your body temperature just went up." (Is that amazing or what?!) Though he always thought that God was for him, Mike said that in that moment, he knew that he knew that he knew that God had his best interests at heart and that He would take care of him.

Isn't that an incredible story? God can do the same for you too. He would love to hear what's on your heart and what you need from Him.

God wants us coming to Him to ask for things. Obviously, if our motives aren't right or if we are doing something which hinders our prayers, He's not going to grant our request. But He still wants us making requests of Him, whether it's big or small or anywhere in between. God wants us coming to Him expectantly and earnestly. So let's do that—let's ask Him for peace!

 **Takeaway:**
*God wants us talking with Him about everything. When we do this, it brings us peace.*

## Prayer

Father, You are so awesome. I am so thankful that You have made a way for me to communicate directly with You! Please Lord, help me do so more often! Help me to love prayer and hate sin. Help me to be thinking about You all the time so that I can come to You about anything, anytime (simply, continually, small, big). Help me to pray persistently and expectantly. And please reveal to me anything that might be hindering my prayers. Amen.

# THIRTEEN

# Focus on the Good

*Finally, brothers, whatever is true, whatever is noble, whatever is right,*
*whatever is pure, whatever is lovely, whatever is admirable—if anything*
*is excellent or praiseworthy—think about such things.*
*(Philippians 4:8)*

*"Instead of complaining that the rosebush is full of thorns, be happy*
*that the thorn bush has roses."*
*German Proverb*

One thing I have done in some of my workshops or talks is to take a blank white sheet of paper and draw a dot on it, right in the center. While holding it up for the audience, I ask them what they see. One hundred percent of the time, I hear, "A dot!"

Why is it that we focus on the dot? They could easily say, "I see a lot of white space," and that would make sense, because the vast majority of the page is white and unblemished. Yet, we have a tendency to focus on the dot. Not just in this exercise, but in life.

This is so clear to me when I am standing on the back end of some dots, or problems, I have encountered in my life. Had I focused on the big picture, or the white space, rather than the problem, or the dot, my situation might have cleared up much quicker. It at least would have been more peaceful while I was going through it.

One of my favorite promises in God's Word is found in Romans 8:28, *And we know that in all things God works for the good of those who love him, who have been called according to his purpose.*

I believe in what this verse is saying, yet my actions often reveal that, deep down, I don't. If I really knew, at the core of my being, that God was going to turn my dot into something good, I can guarantee you that I wouldn't be so uptight during certain times.

My past has shown me repeatedly that this verse is true, that God does work ALL things out for good for those who love Him, who have been called according to His purpose. But, many times, I focus on the dot. How about you?

If you find that you tend to be a "dot-watcher," take heart; you're not alone. Even some of the great Biblical leaders had this issue. Consider Jesus' 12 disciples:

> During the fourth watch of the night Jesus went out to them, walking on the lake. When the disciples saw him walking on the lake, they were terrified. "It's a ghost," they said, and cried out in fear.
>
> But Jesus immediately said to them: "Take courage! It is I. Don't be afraid."
>
> "Lord, if it's you," Peter replied, "tell me to come to you on the water."
>
> "Come," he said.
>
> Then Peter got down out of the boat, walked on the water and came toward Jesus. But when he saw the wind, he was afraid and, beginning to sink, cried out, "Lord, save me!"
>
> Immediately Jesus reached out his hand and caught him. "You of little faith," he said, "why did you doubt?" (Matthew 14:25-31)

Can you see all the dot-watching going on in this passage? First, "they were terrified" and fearfully said, "It's a ghost." Obvious dot-watching. Then one of them had the guts to show some faith, step out of the boat, and begin to walk on water. Then a big dot came into Peter's focus. He began to focus on the wind instead of Jesus and he began to sink.

Am I suggesting that we need to ignore our dots, or our issues and problems? Not at all. Obviously we need to pay *some* attention to the negatives in our lives. However, if that is all we focus on, we will be in trouble. Dot watching will always cause us problems if we don't keep the bigger picture in focus. If we continually bombard our minds with bad stuff, we are guaranteed to have a lack of peace.

I'm sure you know some really negative people—we all do. Someone I know went on a cruise to the Hawaiian Islands with his wife. It was their "dream vacation." When he returned I asked him, "Hey Frank (not his real name), how was Hawaii?"

Frank responded, "It was okay. But the boat wasn't new and the people on the cruise were very rude. In fact, I was standing in line for the buffet when this couple just cut right in front of me. When I asked them what they were doing they said something very nasty to me!" This negativity went on for several minutes with not one word about the incredible scenery, the fantastic weather or the time spent alone with his wife.

I felt sorry for him. He had just returned from a trip that most people can only dream of. He was in one of the most beautiful places on this earth and all he could focus on were the negative parts of the trip, which took away his peace and joy. Very sad, but a very true reality for many of us.

How do you feel after spending time with people like this? If you're like me, you're drained and maybe even a bit depressed. That's the same way I feel if I lay around watching TV. I feel crummy. Garbage in, garbage out. I think that's what Paul was trying to get through to us in Philippians 4:8.

Consider the story of a man leaving one town and headed for another. Before reaching his destination, he encounters a fellow sitting along the roadside and asks him, "What's it like in the town ahead? Are the people friendly? Is the economy good?"

The fellow answers him with questions of his own: "What was it like in the town you just left? Were the people friendly? Was the economy good?"

The traveler snapped back, "Of course not, you fool. That's why I'm leaving. The people were dumb and cheap and bad to do business with and the economy was awful."

The fellow said, "I see. Well, I have bad news for you. The town up ahead is just like the one you left."

An hour or so later, another, different traveler comes along, encounters the same fellow sitting by the side of the road, and asks him the same questions about the town ahead. Again, the fellow asks him, "What was it like in the town you just left? Were the people friendly? Was the economy good?"

The traveler smiled and said, "Why yes, everybody was kind and friendly and generous and the economy was quite good."

The fellow said, "I have great news. The town up ahead is just like the one you left."

Which traveler do you think has more peace?

I have heard it said that humans cannot have opposing thoughts in their head at the same time. Yes, you can switch back and forth, but at the exact moment in time, you cannot be both loving and hateful—it's impossible.

So when faced with challenges, you can choose to magnify God or magnify your troubles, but you cannot magnify both.

## But Dad!

"But Dad! I don't wanna do it!"

That may be the universal whine from children, pre-programmed to intensify at adolescence. At least it has been this way at times in my household (either coming from my children or coming from me when I was younger). At the time of this writing, my son, Robert, is 15 years old and he has adopted this mantra of late, much to my chagrin. Though I don't like it, I know it is actually doing more harm to him than to me.

In Philippians 2:14, Paul encourages us to, *Do everything without complaining or arguing*. There's a pretty important word in there, *everything*. Paul's not telling us to not complain or argue only when we do certain things, like play video games—that'd be easy, at least for Robert. No, he is saying in *everything*. Even helping your dad who sometimes doesn't understand 15-year-olds.

We had a recent occurrence with Robert and he has graciously allowed me to share it with you. I had four cubic yards of topsoil delivered to my house for a landscaping project. This was no small pile. In fact, I checked online and found out that, because it was wet due to a recent rain, it weighed over five tons!

So Robert and I took a couple of shovels and a wheelbarrow and ventured outside to tackle this. We shoveled dirt. We wheeled dirt— is that what one does with a wheelbarrow? And we spread dirt. This went on for about five "wheelbarrows full" and we both were a bit discouraged. It seemed like we hadn't even put a dent in the pile of dirt situated on my driveway.

Upon seeing this, Robert said, "How much are we going to do today?"

I said, "We're going to get as much done as we can." A very encouraging answer don't you think? From Robert's perspective, knowing his crazy dad, he probably thought we were going to work through the night. He became discouraged and said, "But Dad, I don't wanna do anymore!"

This led to a "discussion" and then Robert shut it down. He refused, no matter what, to do any more. In fact, he said to me, "What are my consequences if I don't do anymore?" I told him some pretty severe consequences and he opted to go inside.

(Truthfully, I asked him to go inside after a little complaining because I didn't want to hear anymore of his attitude.) He did "serve his time" and face consequences, but this showed me something.

He was so focused on the enormity of the task and the fact that it wasn't a lot of fun, that he lost all sight of the big picture. He was clearly focusing on the dot and was arguing and complaining. He became so focused on that dot, that, even when faced with some pretty negative consequences, he chose a path that led to more pain.

I ended up moving the majority of that topsoil over a two-day period myself. When the job was completed, I felt a great deal of satisfaction and pride in my work. It felt good. And you know what? I also felt peaceful.

Robert could have felt this, too, had he chosen a different attitude regarding his work.

This encounter got me to wondering how my dad ever put up with me, because I acted much the same way when I was Robert's age. So perhaps I, too, could have had more peace in my life had I followed what Paul exhorts us to do in Colossians 3:23-24: **_Whatever_** _you do, work at it with all your heart, as working for the Lord, not for men, since you know that you will receive an inheritance from the Lord as a reward. It is the Lord Christ you are serving_ (emphasis added). Perhaps one of the reasons for this advice is so we can be more peaceful.

## The Tough Boss

In my first book, _Bleedership: Biblical First-Aid for Leaders_, I shared about a very difficult boss I had who made our lives miserable. I was Vice-President of Sales for this company and had 25 sales people who reported to me.

During that season in my life, I probably got more things wrong than right, but occasionally I would get something right. In one such instance, my boss called me and four of our salespeople into a meeting to explain how we had violated a bunch of his rules. For much of the three-hour meeting, he was in my face screaming obscenities with such intensity that I could see the veins bulging in his neck.

A few days prior to this, my wife and I attended our regular Bible study group. The topic that evening was fear, or rather, the phrase "fear not" which appears a lot in the Bible. In our discussion, one verse really stuck out for me:

> My soul finds rest in God alone; my salvation comes from him. He alone is my rock and my salvation; he is my fortress, I will never be shaken. (Psalm 62:1-2)

I found myself meditating on this verse prior to our meeting. Even in the midst of his tirade, I was actually repeating to myself, "He is my fortress, I will never be shaken." I found myself not only feeling extremely calm, but filled with confidence also. I was then saying to myself, "He is my fortress, I will never be shaken. Bring it on—I can take it!"

Normally if treated this way, even by my boss, I would have been agitated and responded angrily. However, in this case, I was as cool as a cucumber. For some reason, the fact that my boss couldn't get to me made him even angrier which made the whole thing kind of fun.

The level of peace I experienced that day is attributed to two things. First, I was using the Word of God as a weapon (it is referred to as the *sword of the Spirit* in Ephesians 6:17). And second, I was thinking about what was true, noble, right, praiseworthy, pure, etc... I was pondering good things!

## Me, Myself and I

When things are tough in your life, who are you thinking about most of the time? Be honest now. It's *you*, right? Sure it is. If I'm honest, even when things are going *well*, I'm thinking about *me* most of the time. Ever since Adam and Eve brought sin into the world, we human beings have been a selfish lot. We are born that way.

Think about a young toddler playing with some of her toys. Picture another child coming onto the scene and grabbing one of her toys so he can join in on the fun. What does she typically say? "Mine!" I don't know a parent who has taught their child that, at least intentionally. Yet, almost every child says the same thing, "Mine!" Let's face it: we are selfish.

So what does this have to do with pondering good things and peace? I have seen that when I (or others I know) wallow in self-pity and only think about myself, I can get to a place of depression or at least feeling down about things. Yet, when I have been able to break through that feeling and focus on someone else and how I might help them, it does something in my mind and in my heart. I have a renewed bounce in my step. I have purpose. I have more peace. Perhaps it is because I simply have taken my mind off my issues and me. Or perhaps, it is because I am doing what God wants me to do and I am getting away from that *stinkin' thinkin'*, which includes thinking only about me.

> A group of graduates, well established in their careers, was talking at a reunion and decided to visit their old university professor who was now retired. During their visit, the conversation turned to complaints about stress in their work and lives. Offering his guests hot chocolate, the professor went into the kitchen and returned with a large pot of hot chocolate and an assortment of cups: porcelain, glass, crystal, some plain looking, some expensive, some exquisite. He told them to help themselves to the hot chocolate.
>
> When they all had a cup of hot chocolate in hand, the professor said, "Notice that all the nice-looking, expensive cups were taken, leaving behind the plain and cheap ones.

While it is normal for you to want only the best for yourselves, that is the source of your problems and stress. The cup that you're drinking from adds nothing to the quality of the hot chocolate. In most cases, it is just more expensive and in some cases even hides what we drink. What all of you really wanted was hot chocolate, not the cup; but you consciously went for the best cups...and then you began eyeing each other's cups.

"Now consider this: life is the hot chocolate; your job, money and position in society are the cups. They are just tools to hold and contain life. The cup you have does not define, nor change the quality of life you have. Sometimes, by concentrating only on the cup, we fail to enjoy the hot chocolate God has provided us. God makes the hot chocolate, man chooses the cups. The happiest people don't have the best of everything. They just make the best of everything that they have. Live simply. Love generously. Care deeply. Speak kindly. And enjoy your hot chocolate."

## You Hit Where You Aim

In Chapter 3, I told the story of the famous motivational speaker who was trying his hand at driving on a NASCAR track. He had a tendency to want to look at the concrete wall as he was driving, much to the dismay of his coach. His coach knew that what he should focus on was where his car would go.

The same thing is true with the negative circumstances in life. If we continually focus on them, if we wallow in our pity, if we complain and argue and we lose sight of the bigger picture, how can we expect to be anything but miserable? If we focus on the wall, we are going to hit it sooner or later.

In the book of Hebrews, the heroes of the faith are described in chapter 11. This is referred to by many as *God's Hall of Fame*. After mentioning these individuals by name, the author of Hebrews says this:

All these people were still living by faith when they died. They did not receive the things promised; they only saw them and welcomed them from a distance. And they admitted that they were aliens and strangers on earth. People who say such things show that they are looking for a country of their own. *If they had been thinking of the country they had left, they would have had opportunity to return.* Instead, they were longing for a better country—a heavenly one. Therefore God is not ashamed to be called their God, for he has prepared a city for them. (Hebrews 11:13-16, emphasis added)

Did you get that? If they had been thinking of the country they had left, they would have had opportunity to return. In other words, if their mind was not focused on the right thing, they could have easily been taken off course. To simplify it further, you hit where you aim.

I like the answer a 104 year-old woman gave when she was asked what it's like to not have her friends around anymore: "There's no peer pressure!"

So let's be like this woman and look on the bright side of things. Let's agree to think about:

- whatever is true;
- whatever is noble;
- whatever is right;
- whatever is pure;
- whatever is lovely;
- whatever is admirable;
- anything that is excellent or praiseworthy.

## No Worms

A minister decided that a visual demonstration would add emphasis to his Sunday sermon.

Four worms were placed into four separate jars.

The first worm was put into a container of alcohol.

The second worm was put into a container of cigarette smoke.

The third worm was put into a container of chocolate syrup.

The fourth worm was put into a container of good clean soil.

At the conclusion of the sermon, the minister reported the following results:

- The first worm in alcohol—Dead;
- The second worm in cigarette smoke—Dead;
- The third worm in chocolate syrup—Dead;
- The fourth worm in good clean soil—Alive.

So the minister asked the congregation, "What did you learn from this demonstration?"

Maxine, who was sitting in the back, quickly raised her hand and said, "As long as you drink, smoke and eat chocolate, you won't have worms!"

That story made me smile. I love Maxine's spunk and I have to give Maxine credit; she is focusing on what is "right" in her mind. However, when Paul was instructing us to think about whatever is right, or true, or noble, or praiseworthy, and so on, he wasn't encouraging us to come up with our own list of what is right or true.

He is instructing us that there is one Truth and that we have been given instructions as to how to live...in God's Word. In Romans 12:2 Paul tells us to be "transformed by the renewing of your mind." In other words, transformation begins when we change our thinking. So we are *to really focus on* what God thinks is true, noble, right, pure, lovely, admirable, excellent and praiseworthy. The only way to do this is to spend time with Him in His Word and to spend time with others discussing His truths.

**Takeaway:**
We must choose to think about what is good and praiseworthy rather than dwelling on the bad, worrisome stuff.

## Prayer

Father, You are so cool! Thank You for Your creation—there is so much good all around me! Help me focus on that goodness, on the positive stuff rather than the "dot" or the problems. I know that dots will be all around but I also know that the good stuff You have blessed me with is so much greater than my problems. Help me focus on the truly important things in my life. Especially help me to focus more on You so that You can reveal to me what is important to You. Amen.

# Peace For You

This concluding section begins by looking into a very practical and necessary part of the peace process. We will also look at some of Jesus' warnings to us and then we will step together onto the pathway to peace.

Here is what we will explore in the coming chapters...

# FOURTEEN

# Prayerful Planning

*The plans of the diligent lead to profit*
*as surely as haste leads to poverty.*
*Proverbs 21:5*

*"There are two ways to sleep well at*
*night—be ignorant or be prepared."*
*Simon Black*

T his chapter is probably going to leave some of you upset and claiming heresy against yours truly. Some might be saying, "We can't make plans, only God can!" or "Planning is leaving God out of the process." If you are in this camp, here is a verse that seems to back up your point of view:

> In his heart a man plans his course, but the LORD determines his steps. (Proverbs 16:9)

If this were the only verse we looked at, I might agree with you that planning is not our job. However, as I read Scripture, I see that we are called on to make plans. Here is a verse to supports this:

> Make plans by seeking advice; if you wage war, obtain
> guidance. (Proverbs 20:18)

That verse is telling us how to make plans, which clearly means we are to make plans.

I've heard it said that the best way to make God laugh is to tell Him our plans. Yet it appears that God clearly wants us to plan. So what gives? Do we plan or don't we? It is clear to me that we are to plan but we must do so with God. We must prayerfully plan:

> Commit to the LORD whatever you do, and your plans
> will succeed. (Proverbs 16:3)

Here we learn that one of the keys to effective planning is committing our plans to the Lord. One way I like to view this is that I can make plans all day long, but God can decide to modify those plans at any time. When I get in trouble is when I try to hang onto my plans when He has something else in mind. I am a work in progress on this and I am so thankful for the grace He has given me here. However, though I don't act like it at times, I know that His plans trump my plans every time. And, they trump your plans, too.

Consider an interesting passage from Paul's letter to the Romans:

> I do not want you to be unaware, brothers, that I planned
> many times to come to you (but have been prevented from
> doing so until now) in order that I might have a harvest
> among you, just as I have had among the other Gentiles.
> (Romans 1:13)

Clearly, Paul made plans, and in this case, his plans were repeatedly dashed. Yet, that did not stop him from planning.

Oswald Chambers has this to say on this subject in *My Utmost*

*For His Highest*: "All our fretting and worrying is caused by planning without God."[1] Notice, he didn't say that all our fretting and worrying is caused by planning, only planning *without* God.

## Joshua the Planner

Let's look at a story...

> Then the LORD said to Joshua, "Do not be afraid; do not be discouraged. Take the whole army with you, and go up and attack Ai. For I have delivered into your hands the king of Ai, his people, his city and his land. You shall do to Ai and its king as you did to Jericho and its king, except that you may carry off their plunder and livestock for yourselves. Set an ambush behind the city."
>
> So Joshua and the whole army moved out to attack Ai. He chose thirty thousand of his best fighting men and sent them out at night with these orders: "Listen carefully. You are to set an ambush behind the city. Don't go very far from it. All of you be on the alert. I and all those with me will advance on the city, and when the men come out against us, as they did before, we will flee from them. They will pursue us until we have lured them away from the city, for they will say, 'They are running away from us as they did before.' So when we flee from them, you are to rise up from ambush and take the city. The LORD your God will give it into your hand. When you have taken the city, set it on fire. Do what the LORD has commanded. See to it; you have my orders." (Joshua 8:1-8)

Joshua models this very concept to us here. First, he hears from God and gets direction. So far, so good. However, had this been all he did, I believe he and his troops would have been in trouble. God gave him orders to attack, but He left out the majority of the details. God told Joshua the direction he should go, He just didn't give him the plans to get there.

So Joshua clearly had to plan the details out so that God could partner with him in this battle. He had faith in God for the outcome but he also knew he needed to do his part.

Imagine, if you will, Joshua going to war against Ai without a battle plan. Can you picture the chaos that would have ensued? Do you think Joshua would have been at peace? No, I don't think so.

Years ago a friend of mine received notice that his home was being foreclosed on. At the time, his life was an absolute mess. His wife had left him, he was out of work and not really interested in finding a job, and his health was in serious jeopardy. He was also battling depression, which was understandable.

Just 27 days before he was to be out of his house, two others (including his pastor) and I went to him to see how we could help and to offer some encouragement. I asked, "What is the plan to get your stuff out of your house?"

He said, "Now that's the difference between you and me. You're a planner and I'm not. I'm feeling good about things right now so I'm just going to do my best and God will work it out."

His pastor said, "Failing to plan is planning to fail."

Because he did not want to hear that he dismissed it. As a result, we left without a plan to help him. Then, three days before he had to leave the house, he called me and I could sense the utter panic in his voice as he said, "Jim, I don't know what I'm gonna do. I need to be out of here in three days and I haven't done anything!"

If there were such a thing as a peace scale that measured the amount of peace in a person on a scale of 1 to 10, my friend would have been at negative 50. He had no peace. Zero. Zip. Nada. He was running on fumes. He did end up making it through those times but the fact remained that he had no peace at that time. A big reason for that was that he had no plan.

I share this story with you not to bash my friend, but rather to help you. I have heard it said that a smart person learns from his own mistakes while a wise person learns from the mistakes of others. I am hopeful that this illustration can be something to help you avoid the same sort of mistake in your life.

This planning thing is not just for big stuff in our lives. Planning is essential in just about everything including our money, our time, how much sleep we get, what we want to do for fun and when we're going to put gas in our car.

As of this writing, the road from my office to my favorite restaurant for lunch is under construction. As a result, anytime I have a meeting there, it takes me an extra five minutes or so to arrive.

Last week I was to meet a friend there and was working away in my office, trying my best to get some things done. I set a goal to complete some tasks, which would have been better to do after lunch. However, I wanted to be "productive." This led me to leave five minutes later than I should have.

On the way to my appointment, I was kicking myself for my poor planning. I didn't leave myself enough time and I was very anxious on my way. To make matters worse, I left the person's cell phone number in my office so I couldn't even call them to let them know I was going to be late. And of course, it seemed like there were extra dump trucks on the scene making my drive even slower. Ugh!

Even though I knew the person I was meeting would understand, I was still very stressed about it. I hate to be late as I feel that is telling the other person that my time is more important than his or hers is.

From a relative perspective, this is a very small thing and many could say that the construction caused me to be late. In a way, this was true, but because I was aware of it in advance, it was really my poor planning which caused me to be late. My poor planning caused me to have very little peace on my drive.

Jesus may be at the center of your life. You may know in your heart that God wants you to have peace and that it is readily available to you. You may have a heart bent toward righteousness. In addition, you might be pondering good things, exulting and rejoicing, being thankful, praying regularly and you may be considerate to others. You may have also declared that you are no longer going to let anxiety rule you, that you are eliminating anxiety. Even if you have done all that, if you fail to plan, I don't believe you can have the peace of God which transcends all understanding.

Jesus shares with us in a brief but powerful parable about the importance of planning before building a tower:

> "Suppose one of you wants to build a tower. Will he not first sit down and estimate the cost to see if he has enough money to complete it? For if he lays the foundation and is not able to finish it, everyone who sees it will ridicule him, saying, 'This fellow began to build and was not able to finish.'" (Luke 14:28-30)

We've all made mistakes in our lives, but think for a second about being the builder of this tower. You excitedly lay the foundation and begin construction of your tower only to find that you've run out of materials. You have no more money so your unfinished work is on display for everyone else to see. You are completely humiliated...and understandably without peace.

Have you ever done something like this? I know I have and I can tell you from experience that it is not peace producing!

## Preparation

My wife is an expert packer for trips. Whenever our family travels, she always anticipates our needs. On a long vacation in the car, we might hear from the back seat, "Mom, do you have a band-aid?"

"Sure honey, it's right here."

Other times it might be, "Mom, do you know where the bug spray is?"

"It's in the bag next to the cooler."

She is amazing. Her thorough preparation truly helps our entire family be more at peace and we are very thankful for that!

## So How Can I Do This?

I have found that when I don't have a plan, I have little hope. My worry muscle begins to flex and I start to think of all the things that aren't healthy for me. I tend to become very anxious.

When I take some time and actually put some thoughts down on paper and look at some possibilities, something incredible happens. I come to a place where I now see great possibilities and I have renewed hope.

When I work with people who are stressed, it is amazing how calming it can be to simply write out all that is on their mind and organize it into buckets. This brings order to the table from a place of confusion. This alone can be a big help.

I was in one of these places recently. I was very confused, stressed and anxious about the direction my life was headed. It seemed like I had too much going on and I thought for sure that I had missed God's direction somewhere along the way.

Bob, a great friend whom I've mentioned previously, sensed my state of despair and offered to sit down with me to help me process everything in my head. We met on a snowy Saturday morning and after some time of worship and prayer, he coached me through the very thing that I have done with others. (Have you ever heard of the shoemaker's son who didn't have shoes? That was me in this case.)

We ended up writing everything down, each point on its own sheet of paper, along with some thoughts others have shared with me. Bob then began to play around with each slip of paper on the table putting it in different configurations. All of a sudden he said, "Look at this!"

When I looked down, I was amazed. It was as if all this confusion in my head instantly vanished. It was now clear. I now had order, or a plan of sorts, for my life.

The funny thing about this is that nothing got eliminated from my life. I still had as much stuff to do. It was just organized a bit differently in my head. I now had a plan. I knew that I didn't need to be stressed or worried about this anymore. I was now at peace. It was very cool. For this, I am very thankful to Bob. He cared enough to come alongside me in my time of need and provided a very valuable service to me. The key to this, though, is that God was very much in the center of our planning process and I know that He guided us exactly where we needed to go.

Moses had someone like this in his life, too. In fact, it was Jethro, his father-in-law of all people:

> The next day Moses took his seat to serve as judge for the people, and they stood around him from morning till evening. When his father-in-law saw all that Moses was doing for the people, he said, "What is this you are doing for the people? Why do you alone sit as judge, while all these people stand around you from morning till evening?"
>
> Moses answered him, "Because the people come to me to seek God's will. Whenever they have a dispute, it is brought to me, and I decide between the parties and inform them of God's decrees and laws."
>
> Moses' father-in-law replied, "What you are doing is not good. You and these people who come to you will only wear yourselves out. The work is too heavy for you; you cannot handle it alone. Listen now to me and I will give you some advice, and may God be with you. You must be the people's representative before God and bring their disputes to him. Teach them the decrees and laws, and show them the way to live and the duties they are to perform. But select capable men from all the people—men who fear God, trustworthy men who hate dishonest gain—and appoint them as officials over thousands, hundreds, fifties and tens. Have them serve as judges for the people at all times, but have them bring every difficult case to you; the simple cases they can decide themselves. That will make your load lighter, because they will share it with you. If you do this and God so commands,

you will be able to stand the strain, and all these people will
go home satisfied." (Exodus 18:13-23)

Jethro intervened to tell Moses what Moses couldn't see, that he
was going to wear himself out and all the people as well. Jethro
helped Moses develop a plan.

Is there someone you know who can help you through stuff like
this? Do you know anyone who could use your help through times
like this? I encourage you to develop relationships like this, relationships where you have a "Jethro" or a "Bob" (or multiple
"Jethros" or "Bobs") in your life and relationships in which you are
able to be one to others.

If you ever get to a place of total confusion, write down your
thoughts and ask the Lord to help you with a plan and to bring
helpers into your life. God is not a God of confusion. He is a God of
order.

As I have mentioned, I am not writing this from a position of
being an expert. I am trying to figure this out in my own life. With
that being said, I can tell you what I've been doing in this area which
has been very helpful for me. I have a desire to take control of the
situations in my life. I want to over-plan everything. As a result, I
need to be intentional about bringing God into my planning process. I recognize that there may be others who will naturally do this
better than I do; I am just explaining the process I go through.

I have found that my best planning happens when I get alone
with the Lord. I have set targets—a plan—to do this daily, weekly,
monthly and annually.

Each morning I like to start my day with God. I try to not make
this a "rule," but most mornings, I spend quiet time praying, reading and listening. Although I haven't always done this, I also find
journaling to be very helpful to me. (To see some ways I've done
this, go to calmingthestormwithin.com/intimacy.) All of this helps
me to be centered on Him as I go about my day. I also mentioned

that when I sit down at my desk I pray for His guidance and that I would only do the things today that He wants me to do. I have found this to be extremely beneficial for me in helping me to know that anything I am planning will only be successful if it's done in concert with God, that I cannot plan apart from Him and that His plans trump my plans. I also try to pray as I'm going about my day.

Every Friday afternoon before leaving my work behind me, I try to assess my next week. I lay out my plan for the week and schedule the important things, which for me might be time with God, time with my wife or kids, time to write and time to exercise. I will also assess what truly needs to be done that week and what can be moved to a future week. Before I began this practice I would often feel pretty anxious about my upcoming week because I felt as if I had way too much to get done and not enough time to do it (which was usually true). Though this takes some time, planning my week has been very helpful to me as my plans are now more realistic and doable. This has helped me have more peace.

In addition to this, I have been spending a two-hour block each week at our local House of Prayer, usually on Wednesdays from 10 a.m. until Noon. During this time I just sit and worship God, pray, read and journal.

Also, once a month I take a day-long retreat. I usually do this on a workday in a remote place. I have been renting a hermitage (a log cabin) for the day on the campus of a college in our community, which has been great. I bring my iPod and begin the day in worship. Then I just do as I feel led. Sometimes I read. Sometimes I talk. I also do a lot of listening, just sitting in God's presence and writing down what He drops into my spirit. I have also brought things with me that need a plan around them along with stuff that I am struggling with. These retreat days have become my favorite day of the month.

Regardless of my surroundings, I have found that when I am intentional about putting God first, I not only get more done, I also tend to get more great ideas and solutions to problems than ever before. Amazing how that works!

Also, at the end of each year I have begun to take a couple of days away from home to assess what my last year looked like from my perspective and from God's. I then look at the coming year to see what I can do differently so that my view and God's can be more closely aligned.

Like I mentioned, I don't have this figured out but I am stepping into it and seeking God. I encourage you to do the same and find what works for you. Ask others for guidance. Then do something!

---

**Takeaway:**
*God is the One who controls outcomes, but He also wants us to plan—without a plan we will not experience the peace God has for us.*

## Prayer

Lord, You are a God of order and I am thankful for that. Lord, I want more order in my life. Please guide me and give me the self-control to take the time to plan with You, even if I don't want to. Help me see the incredible benefits that can come from this. Help me acknowledge You in all my ways so You can make my paths straight. Thank You Lord! Amen.

# FIFTEEN

# Peace Is Yours

*"I have told you these things, so that in me you may have peace."*
John 16:33a

*Whatever you have learned or received or heard from me, or seen in
me—put it into practice. And the God of peace will be with you.*
Philippians 4:9

*"The life of inner peace, being harmonious and
without stress, is the easiest type of existence."*
Norman Vincent Peale

Throughout the gospels, Jesus went from city to city and person
to person doing amazing and miraculous things. This obviously
attracted many to Jesus. Jesus also told them how difficult following Him would be, something many of our churches today are unwilling to do. Here are a few examples from the book of Luke to
illustrate this point:

- "In the same way, any of you who does not give up everything he has cannot be my disciple." (Luke 14:33)
- Then he said to them all: "If anyone would come after me, he must deny himself and take up his cross daily and follow me. For whoever wants to save his life will lose it, but whoever loses his life for me will save it." (Luke 9:23-24)
- As they were walking along the road, a man said to him, "I will follow you wherever you go." Jesus replied, "Foxes have holes and birds of the air have nests, but the Son of Man has no place to lay his head." (Luke 9:57-58)
- He said to another man, "Follow me." But the man replied, "Lord, first let me go and bury my father." Jesus said to him, "Let the dead bury their own dead, but you go and proclaim the kingdom of God." (Luke 9:59-60)
- Still another said, "I will follow you, Lord; but first let me go back and say good-by to my family." Jesus replied, "No one who puts his hand to the plow and looks back is fit for service in the kingdom of God." (Luke 9:61-62)
- Large crowds were traveling with Jesus, and turning to them he said: "If anyone comes to me and does not hate his father and mother, his wife and children, his brothers and sisters—yes, even his own life—he cannot be my disciple. And anyone who does not carry his cross and follow me cannot be my disciple." (Luke 14:25-27)

Though it appears as if Jesus didn't actually want followers, this could not be further from the truth. What He wanted were committed followers who would persevere through the pain and heartache to come. In John 16:33, Jesus warned us that in this life we will have trouble. However, Jesus also promised that with His help we can rise above this trouble and experience peace...the peace which transcends all understanding.

# Warning Signs

Have you ever been stuck on a highway in a traffic jam, not moving at all? If you are like me, this is a terribly frustrating place to be...especially if you're in a hurry to get somewhere. What makes this even more frustrating is when all you see are stopped cars in front of you and you have no idea what's causing the holdup. It might be something as simple as road construction and you could be on your way in five minutes or it's possible there's an accident up ahead and you might be there five more hours...but you don't know. Most of the time it's this uncertainty that causes the most stress.

Before global positioning systems (GPS) were the rage, I used to get a *TripTik* from AAA for our family vacations. These kits would contain all sorts of useful information including a detailed map of the suggested route to our destination. My kids, just as I did when I was younger, used to love to follow along to see how we were progressing on our trip. Unfortunately, this did little to curb the "Are we there yet?" questions but it was still fun for them.

One thing that was especially helpful to me with these maps was that AAA would mark on the map where delays were expected due to road construction. When we encountered a backup in traffic, it was very beneficial for me to know the reason. My frustration level was significantly reduced when I was expecting it in advance because I could then prepare myself, make the best of it, and be more at peace. My preparation could include making adjustments in my expectations of when we might arrive or preparing some activities for my family to do to relieve boredom.

Jesus knows that many of us like to know what lies ahead. As a result, He shared three warnings in John 14-16, some for his disciples and some for all of us. He wants us to be aware and prepared for what is ahead so that we can remain peaceful, even in the midst of difficult circumstances.

### WARNING I: *I'M LEAVING*

- "In my Father's house are many rooms; if it were not so, I would have told you. I am going there." (John 14:2a)
- "You heard me say, 'I am going away.'" (John 14:28a)
- "I will not speak with you much longer, for the prince of this world is coming." (John 14:30a)
- "Now I am going to him who sent me, yet none of you asks me, 'Where are you going?'" (John 16:5)
- "In a little while you will see me no more." (John 16:16a)
- "I tell you the truth, you will weep and mourn while the world rejoices." (John 16:20a)

When Jesus was crucified, most of the disciples fled like roaches in the light. They were obviously frightened and did not immediately get what Jesus was telling them. Though they scattered, they remained close enough to gather together, perhaps because of these words of warning. I wonder what would have become of them had Jesus not given them these warnings of His departure.

Let's take a brief look at each one of Jesus' warnings again because with each one He also delivers hope.

- "In my Father's house are many rooms; if it were not so, I would have told you. *I am going* there *to prepare a place for you.*" (John 14:2 emphasis added)
- "You heard me say, 'I am going away and I am coming back to you.' If you loved me, you would be glad that I am going to the Father, for the Father is greater than I. *I have told you now before it happens, so that when it does happen you will believe.*" (John 14:28-29 emphasis added)
- "I will not speak with you much longer, for the prince of this world is coming. He has no hold on me, *but the world must learn that I love the Father and that I do exactly what my Father has commanded me.*" (John 14:30-31, emphasis added)

- "Now I am going to him who sent me, yet none of you asks me, 'Where are you going?' Because I have said these things, you are filled with grief. But I tell you the truth: *It is for your good that I am going away. Unless I go away, the Counselor will not come to you; but if I go, I will send him to you.*" (John 16:5-6, emphasis added)
- "In a little while you will see me no more, *and then after a little while you will see me.*" (John 16:16, emphasis added)
- "I tell you the truth, you will weep and mourn while the world rejoices. You will grieve, *but your grief will turn to joy.*" (John 16:20, emphasis added)

Can you imagine actually walking alongside Jesus, watching Him turn water into wine, cast out demons, and heal all sorts of maladies? It had to be incredible! For His 12 disciples, this had to be the most thrilling three years of their lives to that point. Here they were, outcasts by society's standard, yet chosen by and in close relationship with the King of kings. Still, Jesus told them that it is for their benefit that He leaves. It had to be very difficult to understand this and in fact, the disciples did not understand these warnings until after His resurrection.

In each of the examples above, Jesus is telling His disciples about a major traffic jam ahead and to be prepared and expectant of it. Not only that, He tells them that this traffic jam is all for good and for their benefit...and our benefit as well!

### WARNING 2: *IF YOU FOLLOW ME, YOU WILL BE HATED AND PERSECUTED*

Who among us doesn't like to be liked? All people do (even though some don't act like it!)—it is universal. That is why Jesus warns us this way:

"If the world hates you, keep in mind that it hated me first. If you belonged to the world, it would love you as its own. As it is, you do not belong to the world, but I have chosen you out of the world. That is why the world hates you." (John 15:18-19)

These are difficult words to hear, especially for us "people-pleasers." Jesus is making it crystal-clear that following Him is by no means the "easy path." He clarifies this even more with this warning:

> "If they persecuted me, they will persecute you also. If they obeyed my teaching, they will obey yours also. They will treat you this way because of my name, for they do not know the One who sent me." (John 15:20b-21)

So not only will we be hated, we will also be persecuted. I have really been wrestling lately with what it means to actually follow Jesus. I have found myself asking these questions to try to determine if I am really a follower. (Perhaps this will help you, too.) Does anyone dislike or hate me because of my devotion to Jesus? Have I been persecuted because of Jesus?

Jesus then intensifies the pressure when He says this:

> "They will put you out of the synagogue; in fact, a time is coming when anyone who kills you will think he is offering a service to God." (John 16:2)

He is stating that at some point in the future, the religious leaders would thrust His disciples out of the synagogue because of their devotion to Jesus. He further shares that they will even be hunted because they are followers of His. Though these words were for the disciples, I am beginning to believe they are applicable to our lives today, as well. I have seen instances in which individuals who have spoken difficult truth in the local church have been asked to leave. Furthermore, there are many Christians who are martyred around the world each day. Whether you believe this to be the case for us now or not, Jesus' warnings are clear: when we follow Him, we probably won't win many popularity contests.

In light of these dire warnings, once again Jesus has good news:

> "Blessed are you when men hate you, when they exclude you and insult you and reject your name as evil, because of the Son of Man." (Luke 6:22)

I remember the first time my son, Robert, wanted to attend an Ohio State football game with me. He was around seven or eight years old. The tickets were expensive and I knew it would be a long day for him. But he really wanted to go and he was quite persistent. I explained to him what the day would look like and the fact that he was probably going to be bored at times. I told him that if he went, I was expecting him to be aware of this and not complain. We attended the game and Robert had a blast. Was he bored at times? Absolutely. Did he complain? Yes, he did. But I really think his complaining was kept to a minimum because he was prepared. In the same way, Jesus is preparing us.

## WARNING 3: *YOU WILL HAVE TROUBLE AHEAD*
"In this world you will have trouble." John 16:33b

Many people I talk to think that when they turn their lives over to Jesus, everything will begin to work out fine. This is clearly not true. Those who follow Jesus will have a more fulfilling life and truly can live life to the full, but Jesus is very clear throughout Scripture that following Him is not easy. He does not sell us. He does not use the old "bait and switch" to persuade us to follow Him. Nope, He tells it exactly like it is. With these warnings of what is to come, we can be more prepared and have more peace while we are in the midst of difficulty. However, there is no escaping that following Jesus will require us to get out of our comfort zones.

## The Danger of Our Comfort Zones

As we begin to receive God's healing from the things that bind us, we start to experience freedom and peace. Then two things tend to happen: we feel the pull of our old way of life and we stop resting in God. When the going gets tough, we tend to resort to what is comfortable, even if it is unhealthy. (This is one of the reasons why accountability is so important in our lives.) Being anxious is one of those "comfortable" things for us. No, we don't like it but we're used to it so it has become comfortable.

We also have a tendency to stop resting in God's freedom. The Israelites and many other Biblical characters didn't rest in this freedom, either. Two of the reasons for this are pride and lack of faith. It was true in Old Testament times and it's true today: we want to create independence because we have a hard time trusting God with our freedom. That's why we work so hard at building up our bank accounts. This self-made security may feel comfortable but it is really robbing us of true peace. To receive true security or peace, we need to do the opposite of what we want to do. We must let go. We must realize that God has the power, not us. He is our only true security.

God wants us to enter the Promised Land. He wants total peace for us. However, we tend to want to walk around in the desert for 40 years like the Israelites, because it is more comfortable. It doesn't have to be this way! We can choose a different path.

If you are serious about seeking peace, I recommend you come to a place where you say, "God, I'm all in. I don't care about my circumstances. Use me as you want." If you can tell that to God truly from your heart, what do you have to be anxious about?

Have you ever heard it said that the safest place to be is in God's will? That's not true. It is the *best* place, but most would agree it is not the *safest* place. Look at Peter. The safest place for him would have been to remain in the boat. He chose the riskier of the options and saw a miracle when he stepped out onto the water because that's where Jesus was.

In the parable of the rich young man (Mark 10:17-31), Jesus told him to sell all his possessions and give to the poor. He said this because the young man's riches were keeping him from being "all in." Jesus is telling us to do away with *anything* that stands between Him and us. Ask God what's keeping you from Him and ask Him to remove that from you. This can be a scary prayer, but remember, Jesus is not in the boat. Jesus came to give us life to the full, including a life filled with peace. If we remain in our comfort zone, we will miss it.

Though I have by no means "arrived," God has done some amazing things in my heart. Over the past several years I've been feeling like I am in over my head professionally and because of the path I've chosen, our ride has not been the most comfortable. I've been way out of my comfort zone. In the past, this would have freaked me out. However, by God's grace I can truthfully tell you that, though I don't know where things are headed, I am more peaceful (and excited) than ever. Again, I'm not where I need to be but thank God I'm not where I used to be!

## The Power of "But"

BUT—a word that typically negates everything previously said. Like, "Honey, you look fantastic, but you could probably stand to lose a few pounds." Or "You did a great job in the game, son, but it sure would have been nice if you would have hit those free throws." The only things heard, or at least focused on, are the words after the "but."

Jesus gave us a huge "but" in John 16:33. "I have told you these things, so that in me you may have peace. In this world you will have trouble. ***But*** take heart! I have overcome the world" (emphasis added).

Had He only said, "I have told you these things, so that in me you may have peace. In this world you will have trouble," that would have been worrisome. But—don't you love that word?!—He didn't. Because He added the BUT, we can all rejoice.

To make it even better, Jesus didn't say, "I am overcoming the world." or "I will overcome the world ." He said, "I *have* overcome the world!" It is done. Finished. Over. He has already done it, which means we don't need to. And, we don't need to worry or be anxious about it, either. Thank You, Jesus! We need to take heart because Jesus has overcome the world!

Jesus does a great job of summarizing the topic of peace in this one powerful verse. Let's look at it one more time:

> "I have told you these things, so that in me you may have peace. In this world you will have trouble. But take heart! I have overcome the world." (John 16:33)

Let's look at what He is saying in these four sentences:
- You will have trouble (so expect it and don't be surprised);
- Take heart (don't be anxious);
- I have overcome the world (why you don't need to be anxious);
- In Me you will have peace (Jesus is the only way).

Very powerful! In that light, I must add that this book is not meant to be a self-help manual or magic formula. Quite the contrary. My hope is that this book will point you directly to Jesus Christ. It is only through Him that we can be transformed, that we can find peace.

## The Cornerstone And Capstone

When a construction crew lays a foundation for a large building, the cornerstone is the first piece put in place. This is the most critical piece, as it will dictate how the rest of the foundation will lay.

The prophet Isaiah told us that God also laid a cornerstone (referring to Jesus) which would provide us with a sure foundation:

> So this is what the Sovereign LORD says:
> "See, I lay a stone in Zion, a tested stone, a *precious cornerstone* for a sure foundation; the one who trusts will never be dismayed." (Isaiah 28:16, emphasis added)

Further, Paul penned these words in Ephesians 2:19-20:

> Consequently, you are no longer foreigners and aliens,
> but fellow citizens with God's people and members of God's
> household, built on the foundation of the apostles and
> prophets, with Christ Jesus himself as the chief *cornerstone.*
> (emphasis added)

So, in seeking peace, if you don't make Jesus the first piece, the
Cornerstone, it will be like building on sand. Jesus told us about
the foolishness in doing this in Matthew 7:26-27:

> "But everyone who hears these words of mine and does
> not put them into practice is like a foolish man who built
> his house on sand. The rain came down, the streams rose,
> and the winds blew and beat against that house, and it fell
> with a great crash."

To look at some additional construction terminology related to
Jesus, consider this verse:

> The stone the builders rejected has become the capstone.
> (Psalm 118:22)

A capstone is the final piece placed on a construction project. In
the above verse, the psalmist is referring to Jesus as the Stone and
the fact that the Jewish leaders, or the builders of the nation, would
reject Him. However, though rejected, God made Jesus the
Capstone, His crowning achievement. This verse is obviously important in God's eyes as it is quoted numerous times throughout
Scripture (see Matthew 21:42, Mark 12:10, Luke 20:17, Acts 4:11
and 1 Peter 2:7).

What God is saying to us is that Jesus is not only the Cornerstone, or the first piece laid in our foundation but He is also the
Capstone, or the last piece laid. In other words He is the beginning

and the end, the Alpha and Omega. Jesus actually refers to Himself this way a couple of times in the book of Revelation.

So it is fitting that He is the first piece *and* the final piece in our quest for peace. In other words, He should be first, last and everywhere in between. God's Word confirms this and tells us that Jesus holds all things together:

> He is before all things, and in Him all things hold together. (Colossians 1:17)

Jesus tells us to "Seek first his kingdom and his righteousness, and all these things will be given to you as well" (Matthew 6:33). "All these things" means <u>ALL</u> these things, including peace. We need to seek Him first in all areas of our life, which then allows Him to be first, last, and in between.

This means going to Him first with everything. This means trusting that He will work out our tough "stuff." This means fully opening our heart and inviting Him to take over, which requires us letting go of control and getting out of our comfort zone.

## Seek First His Kingdom

God's Word is Truth and is filled with promises from Him to us. God cannot break His promises. As we have discovered, God promises us peace and shows us exactly how to get it. However, it doesn't just happen.

When we spend time with God in His Word; when we release control of our lives to God and abide in Him, He transforms us. Jesus had this to say to us in John 15:7:

> "If you remain in me and my words remain in you, ask whatever you wish, and it will be given you."

If we remain in Him and His words remain in us, He will give us whatever we wish, including peace.

So our primary purpose is to seek after God. Abide in Him. Develop an intimate relationship with Him—He so desperately wants that from each of us. Part of doing this is spending time in the Bible. So I encourage you to do this regularly. Set time aside each day to do this. Make it a priority—it will change your life. I can promise you this: marinating in God's Word will transform you and help bring you peace. (Note: for some suggested resources to help you with this, please go to calmingthestormwithin.com/intimacy.)

My hope is that you will use the Scriptures mentioned in this book and that they will become a part of you. (A good one to start with is John 16:33.) Imprint these words from God on your heart and you will begin to notice your life changing in a very positive way. Psalm 119:11 says, "I have hidden your word in my heart that I might not sin against you." We discussed earlier that worry, or anxiety, is really a sin. So hide God's Word in your heart and you will find yourself much less anxious and worrisome...you will be on your way to finding the peace that surpasses all understanding.

Remember the words of Jesus:

> "But seek first his kingdom and his righteousness, and all these things will be given to you as well." (Matthew 6:33)

**Takeaway:**
Following Jesus is not the path to an easy life, yet Jesus is the only way to true, God-given peace. He is the most important piece—He is the beginning and the end.

## Prayer

Father, You are beyond words. I love You so much and I thank You for loving me like You do. I thank You for providing a way to peace. I can see that Jesus is the only way to find that peace, the peace, which surpasses all understanding. And Lord, that's what I want...that's what I am seeking right now. Please forgive me for the times that I have stayed in my comfort zone. Help me, and even challenge me, to break out of that place that I think is safe. Help me to see that it is only outside of my comfort zone where Jesus is. Help me to be like Peter and step out of the boat into the arms of Jesus so I can take hold of the peace, which He has brought me. Finally God, help me to imprint Your words on my heart so that I can have Your peace in me the rest of my days. Amen.

# Appendix A – Free Resources

Here are a few things that you might find helpful:

- The Online Appendix for Calming the Storm Within (including Other Peace Stealers, Prayer Formats and The House of Peace diagram) can be found at: calmingthestormwithin.com/appendix.

- For more information and resources about finding peace: calmingthestormwithin.com/peace.

- If you'd like more information and resources regarding intimacy with God: calmingthestormwithin.com/intimacy.

- To download my Life Planning Assistant: calmingthestormwithin.com/lifeplanningassistant.

- To download my free eBook to help you discover your purpose: calmingthestormwithin.com/purpose.

- For my mom's peanut butter cake recipe: calmingthestormwithin.com/moms-peanut-butter-cake.

- To receive Jim's monthly eight-page magazine for free: 5feet20.com.

# Appendix B – Key Takeaways

**Chapter 1, The Peace I Want:**
*Peace is something provided to us by God (which we need to both seek and receive) that enables us to have tranquility, or be okay on the inside, regardless of our circumstances.*

**Chapter 2, Embrace the Chaos:**
*Chaos is a part of life that cannot be avoided. We need to actually embrace the chaos because God allows it for our own good.*

**Chapter 3, Peace Stealers:**
*Peace isn't stolen from us—we choose to give it up when we refuse to give up control or when we take our eyes off Jesus.*

**Chapter 4, The Path to Peace:**
*The concept of inner peace does not have to be a pipe dream. It is possible and it is something God desires for us...and He has given us a path to follow to peace.*

**Chapter 5, The Only Way:**
God is the God of peace. *The only way to the God of peace is through His Son, Jesus.*

**Chapter 6, Intimacy:**
*Intimacy with our Heavenly Father is critical to finding a life filled with peace.*

**Chapter 7, Obedience:**
*If we willfully disobey God, He will not give us the peace, which transcends all understanding, and we will have to face the natural consequences, which will further hinder our quest for peace.*

**Chapter 8, The Counselor:**
*It is impossible for us to have peace and live the life God has called us to without the help of the Holy Spirit. The Spirit will not do this on His own, but rather will partner with us to bring about this change in our lives.*

**Chapter 9, Joy:**
*We can choose to be joyful in all circumstances and this will help us experience peace.*

**Chapter 10, Gentleness:**
*Being gentle and considerate brings great power and allows us to think more of others than ourselves, which brings peace.*

**Chapter 11, Don't Be Anxious:**
*We can choose to eliminate anxiety and live a life of peace.*

**Chapter 12, Prayer:**
*God wants us talking with Him about everything. When we do this, it brings us peace.*

**Chapter 13, Focus on the Good:**
*We must choose to think about what is good and praiseworthy rather than dwelling on the bad, worrisome stuff.*

**Chapter 14, Prayerful Planning:**
*God is the One who controls outcomes, but He also wants us to plan—without a plan we will not experience the peace God has for us.*

**Chapter 15, Peace Is Yours:**
*Following Jesus is not the path to an easy life, yet Jesus is the only way to true, God-given peace. He is the most important piece—He is the beginning and the end.*

# Resources

## Chapter 1

1) Jim Lange, *Bleedership: Biblical First-Aid for Leaders* (Tate: 2005), p. 112

2) Will Davis Jr., *Pray Big* (Revell: 2007), p. 168

## Chapter 3

1) Eugene H. Peterson, *The Message* (Message: 2002)

2) C.S. Lewis, *The Screwtape Letters* (HarperOne: 2001), p. IX

## Chapter 5

1) Tim LaHaye and Jerry B. Jenkins, *Left Behind* (Tyndale House: 1995)

2) Dale Carnegie, *How To Stop Worrying And Start Living* (Simon & Schuster: 1984), p. 23-25

## Chapter 7

1) "righteousness." Merriam-Webster.com. 2011. http://www.merriam-webster.com (13 Nov 2012).

2) Steve McVey, Grace Walk (Harvest House Publishers: 1995), p.114

## Chapter 10

1) Jerry Bridges, *The Practive of Godliness* (NavPress: 1996), p. 184-185

2) Dale Carnegie, How To Enjoy Your Life and Your Job (Pocket Books: 1990), p. 118

3) John C. Maxwell, *Winning With People* (Thomas Nelson, Inc.: 2007), p. 60-61

## Chapter 11

1) "self-control." Merriam-Webster.com. 2011. http://www.merriam-webster.com (13 Nov 2012).

## Chapter 12

1) Jim Collins, *Good to Great* (HarperBusiness: 2001), p.202

## Chapter 14

1) Oswald Chambers, My Utmost for His Highest: An Updated Edition In Today's Language (Discovery House Publishers: 1992), July 4 devotional

# Are you a doctor or business owner?

Would you like a monthly resource to give to your patients/employees/staff/clients that:
- Encourages them?
- Inspires them?
- Makes them laugh?
- Allows you to minister to them in an easy and non-threatening way?
- Helps them to grow personally and spiritually?
- Contains no advertisements?
- Is customized for your office, which also makes it a great marketing piece?

If you would like to receive a free sample of this 8-page magazine for you to evaluate, go to 5feet20.com/magazine and let me know and I will send it to you right away.

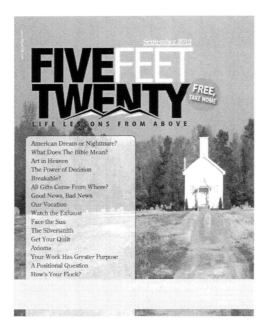

Made in the USA
Lexington, KY
12 December 2012